Winifred Nicholson *in Scotland*

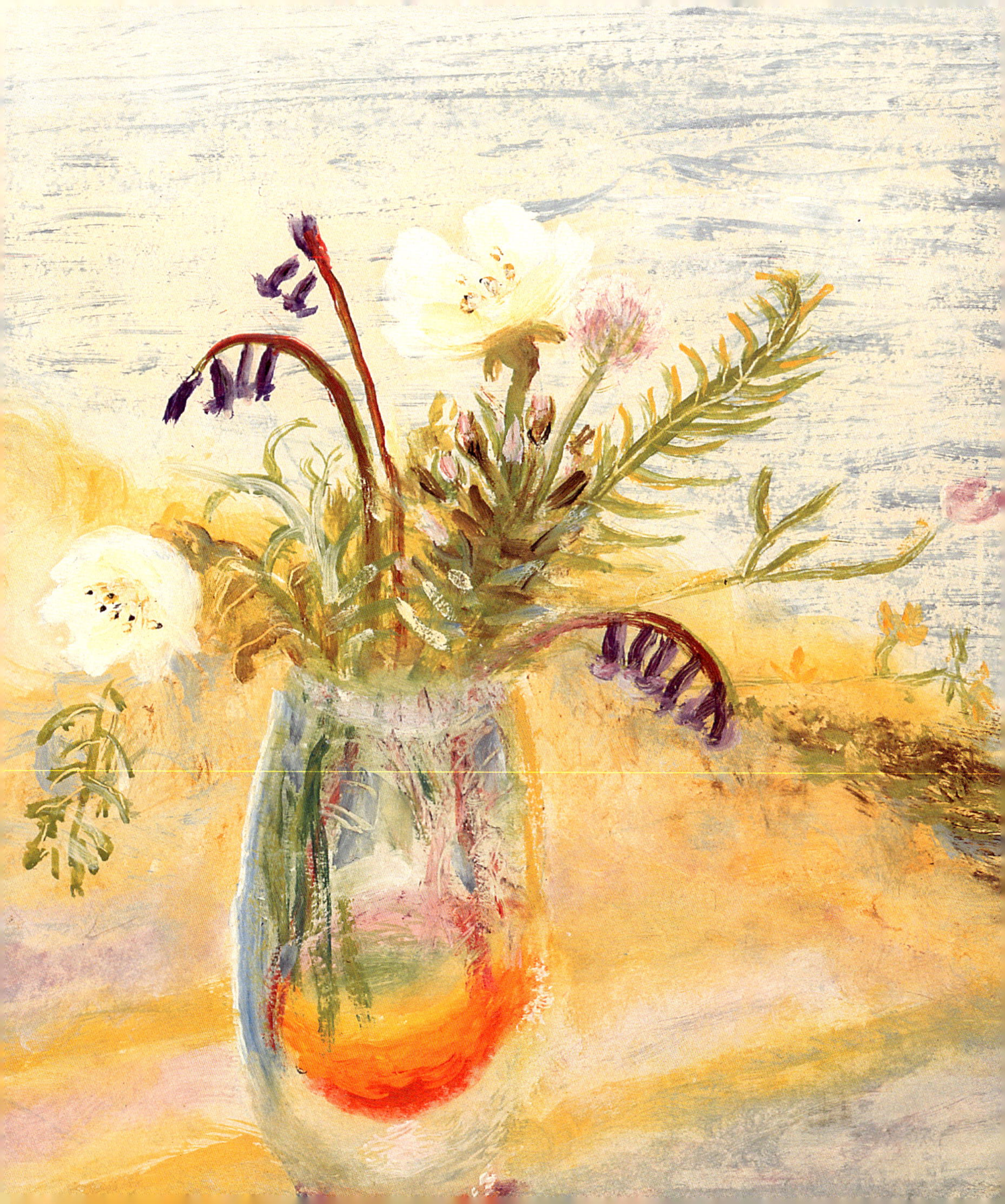

Alice Strang

WINIFRED NICHOLSON
IN SCOTLAND

National Galleries of Scotland
Edinburgh 2003

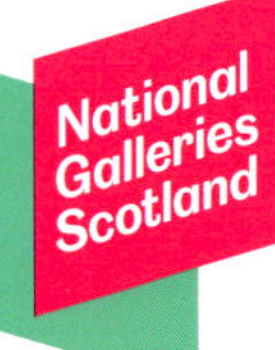

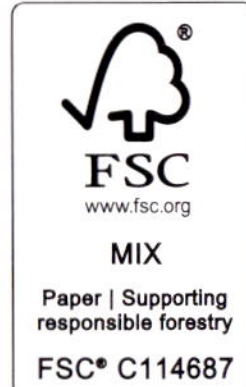

Published by the Trustees
of the National Galleries of Scotland
on the occasion of the exhibition
Winifred Nicholson in Scotland
held at the Dean Gallery, Edinburgh,
10 July – 7 September 2003
and on tour to Duff House, Banff,
8 November 2003 – 18 January 2004
and An Tuireann, Skye,
24 January – 20 March 2004.

Reprinted 2015, 2024

ISBN 978 1 906270 90 2

Designed by Dalrymple
Typeset in Walbaum and Gill Sans
Printed in Great Britain by Gomer Press

Cover illustration:
The Gate to the Isles (Blue Gate) 1980 (detail) Private Collection

Frontispiece:
Hebridean Roses, Eigg 1980 (detail)
Private Collection

FOREWORD

In the late 1940s and throughout the 1950s Winifred Nicholson made frequent working trips to Scotland, often with the poet Kathleen Raine. This book and the exhibition of paintings it accompanies are the first to focus on this aspect of Winifred's oeuvre. She felt a deep affinity with the culture of the Highlands and Western Isles of Scotland and was fascinated by the quality of light created by the ever-changing weather conditions played out over the Scottish landscape.

Not only did Winifred have a special relationship with Scotland, but she also had a particular affection for the Scottish National Gallery of Modern Art. She knew it in its original home in Inverleith House in the Royal Botanic Garden and frequently visited when she came to Edinburgh. Indeed, the painting *Jake and Kate on the Isle of Wight* [plate 1] was presented to the Gallery in 1985 by her trustees in accordance with her wishes. It joined Piet Mondrian's *Composition with Double Line and Yellow* of 1932, which Winifred had previously owned and which the Gallery purchased in 1982.

For their vital help in realising this project we would like to thank Winifred's sons, Jake and Andrew Nicholson and the artist Donald Wilkinson, who accompanied Winifred to Eigg in 1980. Kathleen Raine has kindly given permission for her poems *Shells* and *Love Spell* to be reproduced. Neither exhibition nor publication would have been possible without the generosity of the owners of the paintings, most of whom prefer to remain anonymous. Thanks are also due to Rafaele Appleby, Margaret Fay Shaw, the staff of the Hyman Kreitman Research Centre at Tate Britain, Sally Kalman of Crane Kalman Gallery, London, Peter Milne and Christopher Fleet of the map library of the National Library of Scotland, Jovan Nicholson, Ptarmigan Trust, and Sarah Winlow of the Collections of the National Monuments Record of Scotland at the Royal Commission on the Ancient and Historical Monuments of Scotland. Finally, we are grateful to Alice Strang and her many colleagues at the National Galleries of Scotland, who have enthusiastically brought an idea to life.

We are delighted that the exhibition, *Winifred Nicholson in Scotland*, will tour to Duff House, Banff and to An Tuireann on Skye, an island of which Winifred was extremely fond.

SIR TIMOTHY CLIFFORD
Director-General, National Galleries of Scotland

RICHARD CALVOCORESSI
Director, Scottish National Gallery of Modern Art

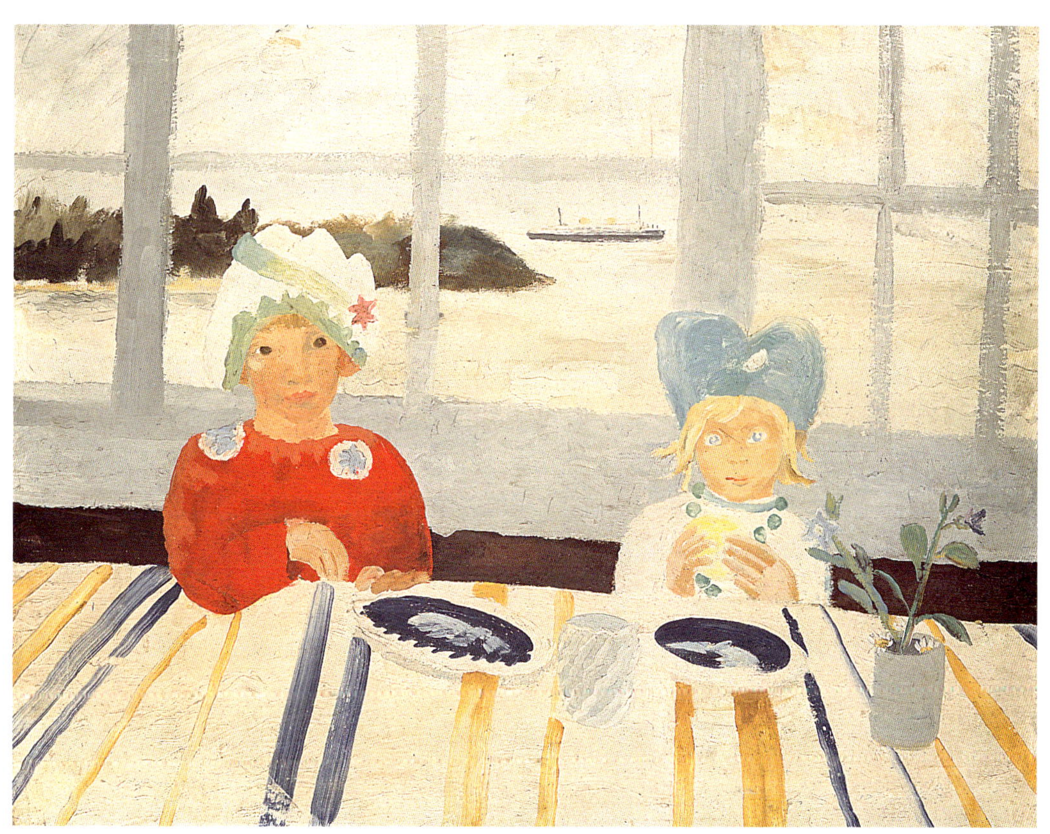

1 **Jake and Kate on the Isle of Wight** 1931–2
Oil on canvas · 68.5 x 89cm
Presented to the Scottish National Gallery of Modern Art, Edinburgh, by the Trustees of Winifred Nicholson's estate in accordance with her wishes, 1985

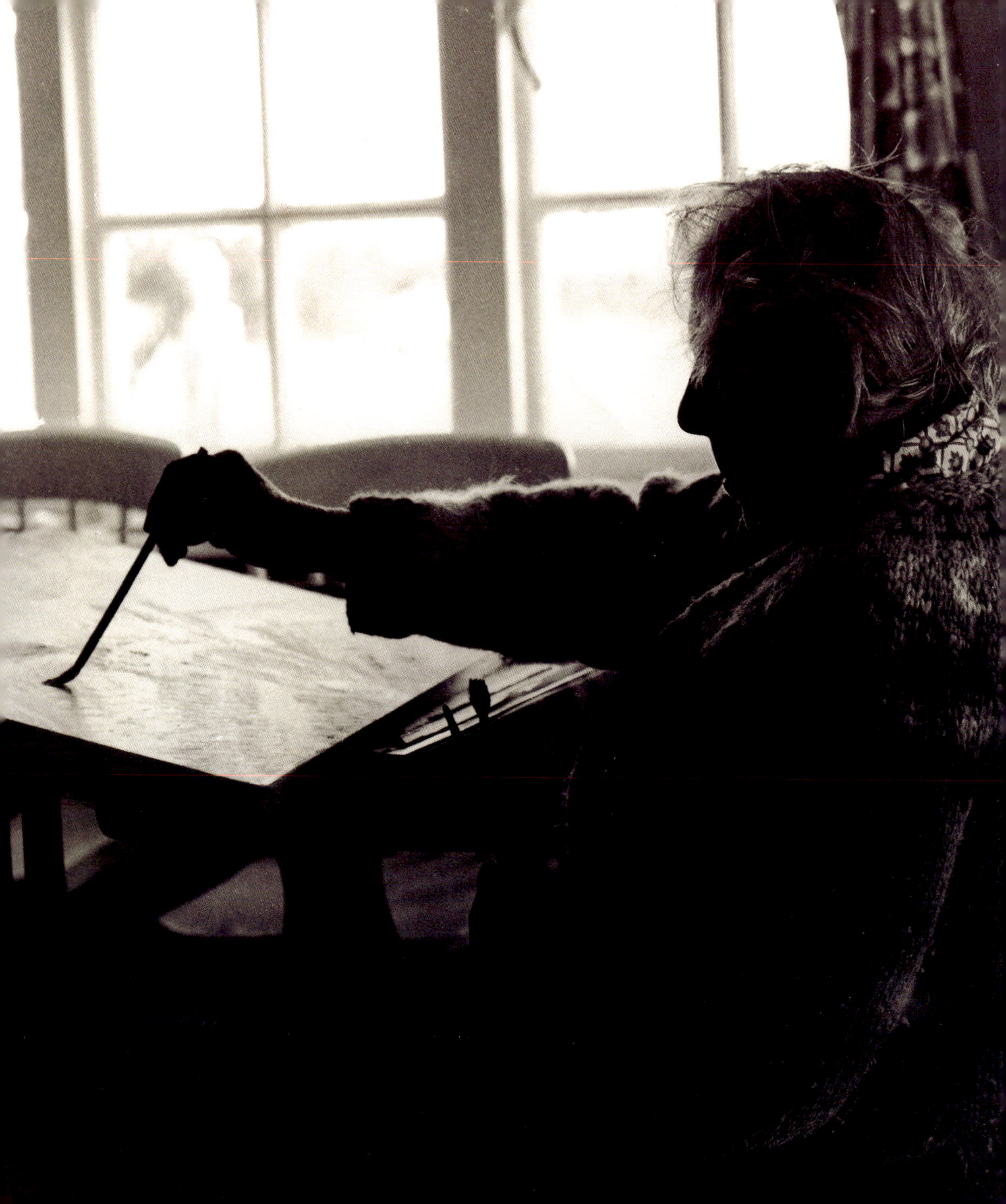

THIS IS THE PLACE AFTER MY HEART

In 1952 Winifred Nicholson (1893–1981) wrote from Sandaig on the west coast of Scotland:

This place looks even more beautiful this year in stormy weather, and is even harder to paint. The high mountains shroud themselves and blot themselves out with white cloud with black cloud with drifting mist and drifting sunshine – the sea is silver is black is azure is lead is white with sea horses, is not visible at all – Kathleen makes the house very gay with dozens of bunches of wild mountain flowers and we have a good fire of sea driftwood. I have painted 4 pictures this week.[1]

Thus Winifred revealed some of the reasons why she made regular working trips to Scotland during the late 1940s and throughout the 1950s, and returned to the island of Eigg in 1980 for what was to be her last such trip. She felt a deep affinity with the Scottish landscape and marvelled at the quality of light and the effects created by the ever-changing weather conditions. She also took a great interest in the history and folklore of the Western Isles and in the traditional way of life of the islanders. When combined with the sympathetic company of friends such as the poet, Kathleen Raine, and a rural lifestyle in remote areas, Winifred found Scotland highly conducive to her work.

Born in 1893 in Oxford, Winifred Roberts was brought up in an artistic milieu. Her mother, Lady Cecilia Maude Roberts (née Howard), was an amateur watercolourist and Winifred's maternal grandfather,

2 Winifred painting *Rhododendrons, Eigg* in the Gamekeeper's Cottage, Eigg, 1980

George Howard, the 9th Earl of Carlisle, to whom she was particularly close, was an artist and friend of many of the Pre-Raphaelites. Winifred studied at Byam Shaw School of Art in London and in 1919–20 spent several months in India with her sister Christina and her father, Charles Roberts, who was Under-Secretary of State for India. The trip had a profound effect on her understanding of colour and light as she noticed 'how eastern art uses lilac to create sunlight' and began to realise that colour could create light, shade and space.[2]

In 1920 Winifred married Ben Nicholson and their mutually influential artistic relationship lasted, despite separation, until Winifred's death in 1981. They lived initially near Castagnola on Monté Bre, in a house that overlooked Lake Lugano. They divided their time between Monté Bre, Paris, London and Cumberland, and travelled widely, keeping abreast of developments in the art world. In 1924 they moved into a seventeenth-century stone farmhouse built on top of a milecastle on Hadrian's Wall, the Roman wall that divides Cumberland from the Scottish Lowlands. This was to remain Winifred's base for the rest of her life.

By the end of the 1920s Winifred was becoming known in British artistic circles and regularly exhibited in London. The death of her close friend, the painter Christopher Wood, in 1930 was followed by Ben Nicholson's decision to leave Winifred and their three young children to live in London with the sculptor, Barbara Hepworth. Winifred's initial response was to take her family to the Isle of Wight, possibly to try to work out why Wood had gone there shortly before his death. From 1932 until 1938 they lived in Paris, enabling Winifred to be at the centre of European Modernism. She already had several contacts in the city, made during earlier trips, and soon became friends with other artists including

César Domela, with whom she studied, Jean Hugo, Jean Hélion, Hans Hartung and Piet Mondrian. She became established as an intermediary between the artistic circles of Paris and London during a time that she later described as 'years of inspiration – fizzing like a soda water bottle'.[3] For a brief period, in addition to her figurative painting, she made purely abstract work which was exhibited under the name Winifred Dacre. Dacre was an old family name and Winifred was encouraged to use it in this way by Ben Nicholson, to avoid confusion between their work.

Due to the increasingly threatening political situation in Europe, in 1938 Winifred accompanied her children to England, before returning to Paris to pack up their apartment. On 21 September, she travelled to London with Mondrian. She spent the war years in comparative artistic isolation in Cumberland, living with her children and her parents in their home, Boothby, and unable to do much painting. She managed a small-holding, ran a school for local children, was secretary of the Northern Goats Society and after the war campaigned vigorously on behalf of the local Liberal Party.[4]

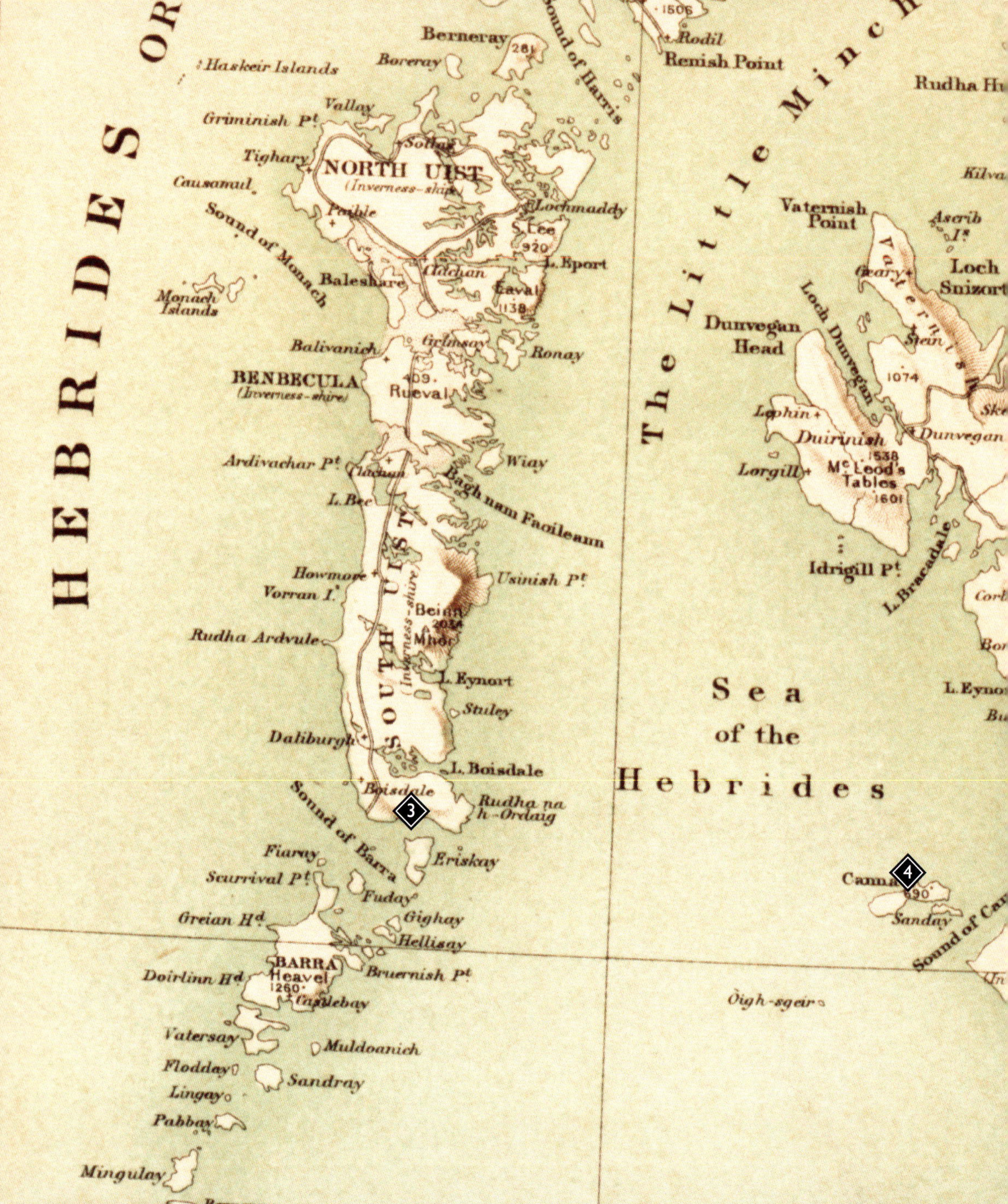

HEBRIDES OR
Haskeir Islands
Berneray
Boreray
Sound of Harris
Rodil
Renish Point
The Little Minch
Rudha H
Valley
Griminish Pt.
Sollas
Tighary
NORTH UIST
(Inverness-shire)
Causamul
Paible
Lochmaddy
Sound of Monach
S. Lee
920
L. Eport
Monach Islands
Baleshare
Clachan
Eaval
1138
Vaternish Point
Ascrib Is.
Loch Snizort
Balivanich
Grimsay
Ronay
Dunvegan Head
Loch Dunvegan
BENBECULA
(Inverness-shire)
Rueval
409
1074
Dunvegan
Lephin
Duirinish
538
Lorgill
McLeod's Tables
1601
Ardivachar Pt.
Clachan
Wiay
Bagh nam Faoileann
L. Bee
Idrigill Pt.
L. Bracadale
Howmore
Usinish Pt.
Vorran I.
SOUTH UIST
(Inverness-shire)
Beinn Mhor
Rudha Ardvule
L. Eynort
Stuley
Sea of the Hebrides
Daliburgh
L. Boisdale
Boisdale
Rudha na h-Ordaig
Sound of Barra
Fiaray
Eriskay
Scurrival Pt.
Fuday
Canna
Sanday
Greian Hd.
Gighay
Hellisay
Sound of Canna
BARRA
Heaval
1260
Doirlinn Hd.
Bruernish Pt.
Castlebay
Oigh-sgeir
Vatersay
Muldoanich
Flodday
Sandray
Lingay
Pabbay
Mingulay
Berneray

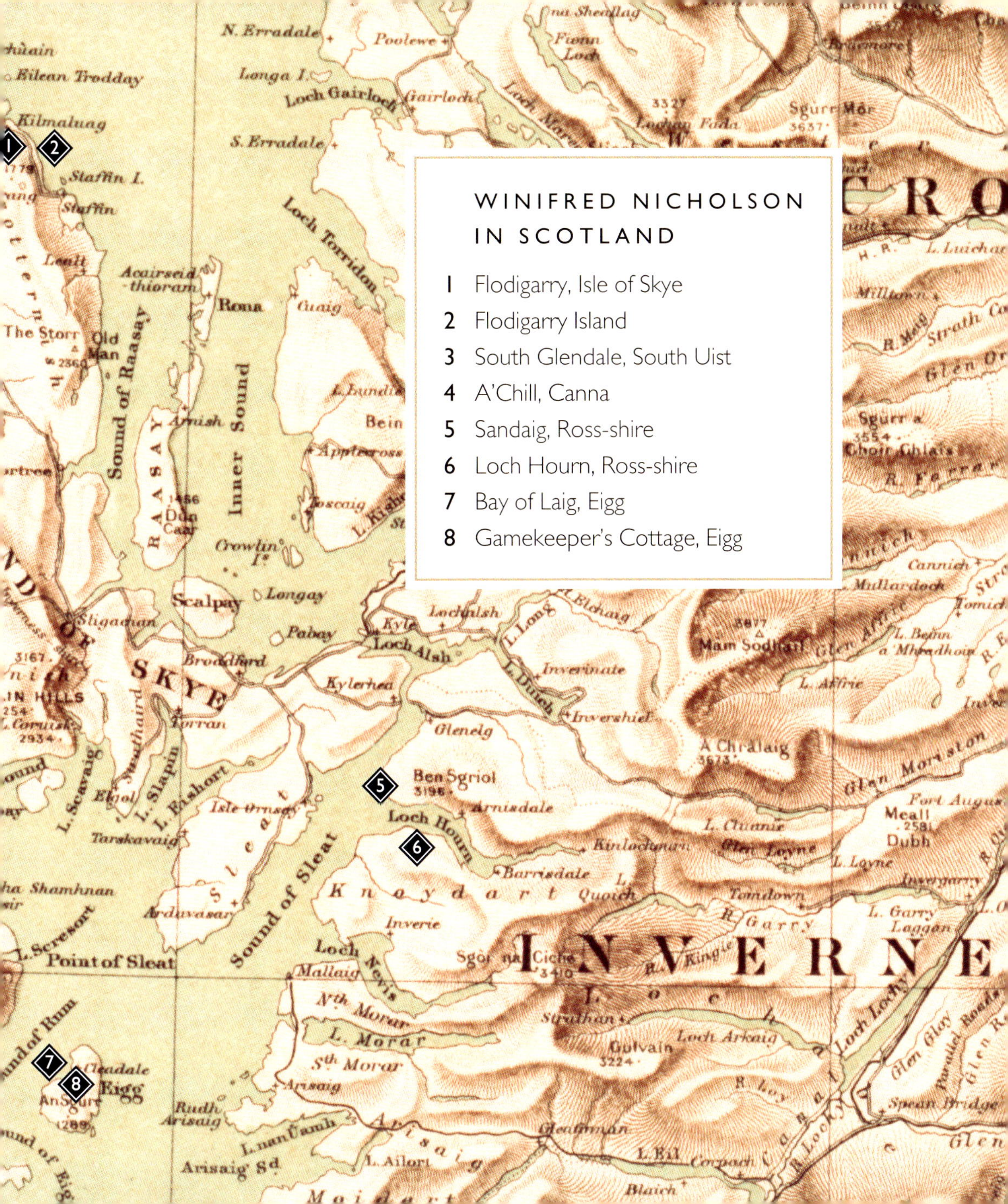

WINIFRED NICHOLSON IN SCOTLAND
1 Flodigarry, Isle of Skye
2 Flodigarry Island
3 South Glendale, South Uist
4 A'Chill, Canna
5 Sandaig, Ross-shire
6 Loch Hourn, Ross-shire
7 Bay of Laig, Eigg
8 Gamekeeper's Cottage, Eigg

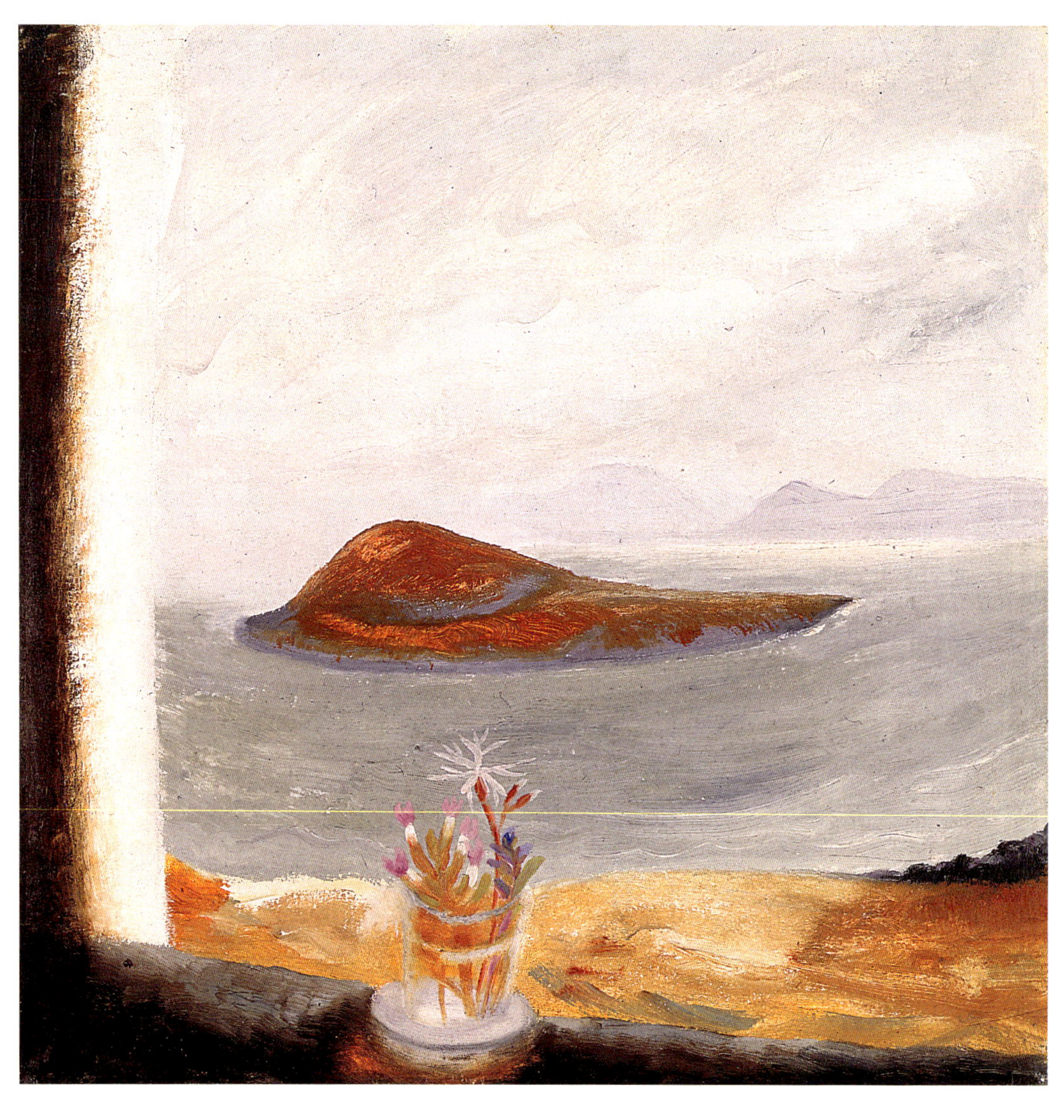

3 *Flodigarry Island, Skye* 1949
Oil on canvas · 61 x 61cm · Kettle's Yard, University of Cambridge

SKYE

Winifred made her first working trip to Scotland, to the island of Skye, in August 1948. Having spent much of her childhood in her grandfather's preferred home, Naworth Castle, a border stronghold in Cumberland, Winifred had always been aware of Scotland. Her adult home was built on Hadrian's Wall itself, the Roman defence between the south and the country which was to become Scotland. Although her family was resolutely English, an interest in the Scots and Celts in general was probably sparked by her grandfather. For example, in 1910 he published *A Picture Song Book*, which shows his interest in Scotland by the inclusion of many Scottish songs, such as 'Border Widow', 'The Bonnie Earl o' Moray' and 'Lochinvar', which are accompanied by his own illustrations.[5] Furthermore, Ben Nicholson's mother, the painter Mabel Pryde, was Scottish. Winifred's children were, therefore, part-Scottish, something which for Winifred, who had a keen sense of personal history, would have been important.

Winifred spent a fortnight on Skye, with her three children, Jake, Kate and Andrew. They stayed in Flodigarry, near the cottage where Flora MacDonald, the Jacobite heroine, had lived. Disguised as an Irish servant girl, Bonnie Prince Charlie escaped in her boat from South Uist in the Outer Hebrides to Skye, pursued by government troops. This kind of romantic history was one of the attractions of Scotland for Winifred.

On Skye, Winifred was finally able to concentrate on her painting, having been able to do very little during the war and its aftermath due to her numerous domestic responsibilities. Before she left Paris in 1938, she had been exploring abstraction in her work, but after the war she returned to representational painting as seen in *Flodigarry Island, Skye* [plate 3].[6] The characteristic composition of Winifred's paintings is a bunch of freshly picked flowers, loosely arranged in a glass jar or modest vase, which is set upon a ledge, often a window sill, with a panoramic view in the distance. However, *Flodigarry Island, Skye* is unusual as in this case the tiny island takes centre stage between the flowers and the distant view of the mainland.

Having painted in the light of India, Switzerland, Cornwall and the Mediterranean, especially the south of France, Winifred was attracted to the gentle light of Scotland, similar to that in Cumberland, and the effects it created over the sea surrounding Skye. She liked northern light because 'the beams fall slantwise, and shine *through* things instead of directly *on* to them as in India or Italy'.[7] Her Scottish palette, as seen in this work, was dominated by tones of silver, grey and green as she strove to capture the changing light in the sky and sea.

The touches of violet amongst the flowers in *Flodigarry Island, Skye* illustrate one of the most important aspects of Winifred's theory of painting. She understood that white light was the source of all colours and that, as seen in rainbows, 'by prismatic action it can be broken into its component rays, each one a distinct colour. Red, orange, yellow, green, blue, violet – a scale line ascending and descending from red hot to violet red.'[8] She thought of the spectrum as a continuous band of colour, repeating itself like octaves on a piano keyboard and as seen in double and triple rainbows. She believed that the scale of colour was incomplete and constantly searched for colours above infrared and below ultraviolet, which are invisible to the human eye. For her the colour violet had special properties, because it lies between the visible and invisible boundary of the colour spectrum. She explained: 'Violet is the colour of highest tension, the colour only visible in its beauty at moments of high vitality and clearest sunlight.'[9] She continued:

It calls to a colour beyond itself on the scale, a colour that our eyes cannot see, although we know that it is there by the power of its ultraviolet rays. Maybe we shall see this colour some day when we have trained our eyes more precisely. Some eyes even now, looking at a rainbow or a prism, can see beyond the violet, a faint trace of fuchsia pink, the indication of the red, the first colour of the rainbow into which the colours flow in their completed cycle. For past the gap where we cannot see, the violet flows back into red again.[10]

Thus the use of violet in *Flodigarry Island, Skye* hints at the component parts and mystery of the light which fills the painting.

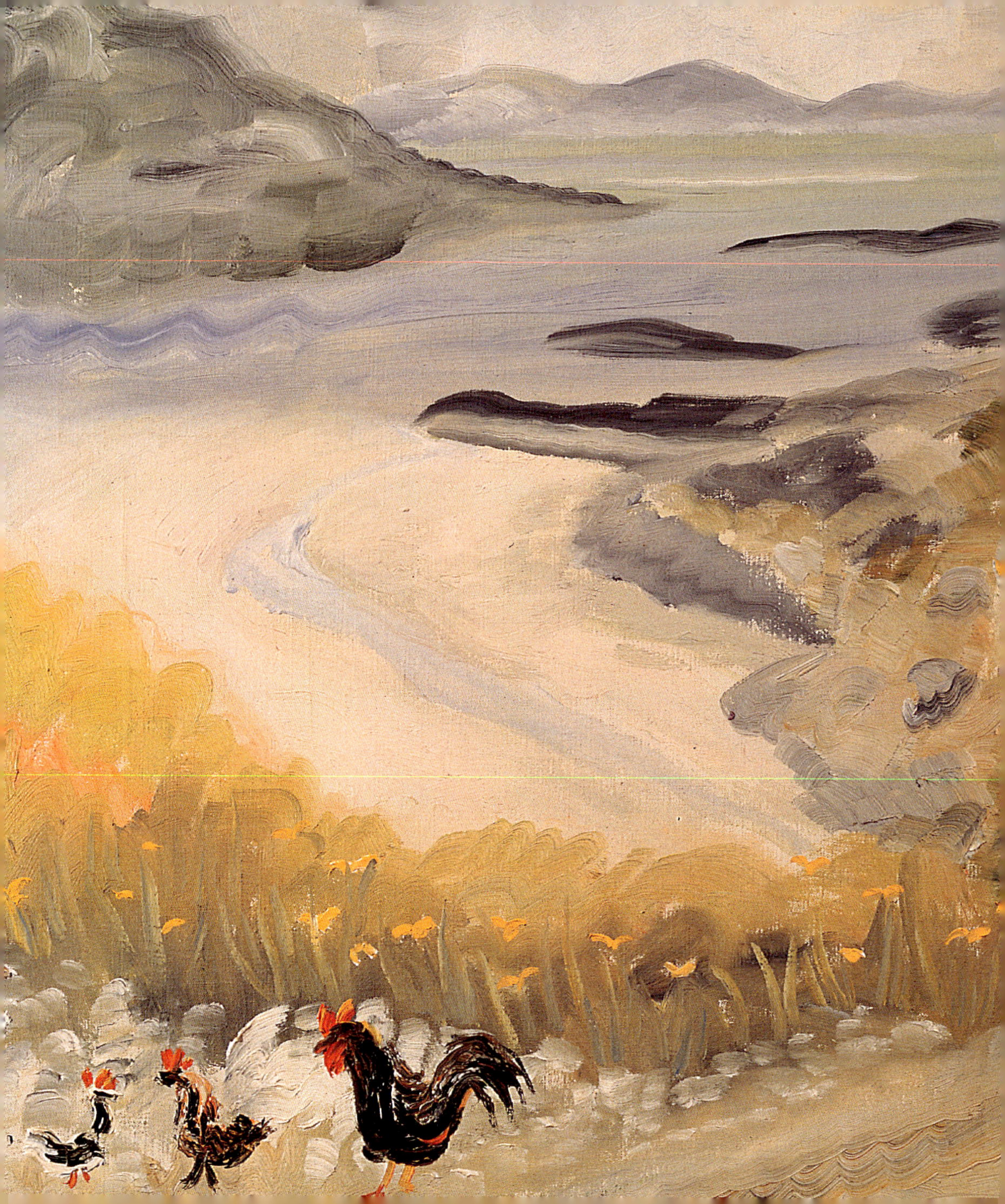

SOUTH UIST

Winifred visited South Uist, in the Outer Hebrides, on at least two occasions; the first was in August 1950 with her children Jake and Kate, when they also spent a week on nearby Barra, and she returned on a later visit with Kathleen Raine. Winifred was attracted to the remoteness of these small islands and regarded reaching them as an adventure. Jake recalls how they took a train from Carlisle, changed at Glasgow, and in the evening reached Oban where they stayed overnight. The next morning they caught the weekly boat to South Uist, which passed through the Sound of Mull, stopping at Tobermory, and then sailed into the Sea of the Hebrides, before finally reaching Lochboisdale. Once there, they caught a bus to the pier on the south end of the island, where no houses could be seen and by which time it was evening. They were met by two fishermen who took them by boat along the coast to South Glendale. Once on land, there was no road so they had to carry their luggage and numerous painting things to a croft where they stayed with the McInnes family.

Winifred described their beautiful, wild and isolated surroundings, and the busy way of life of the crofters, in a letter to her son Andrew:

This is the place after my heart. I wonder if you would like it. Not a tree, not a bush. But grey boulders, grey rocks, grey stones, grey mountains. And bog in between – In the bog, lochs with waterlilies, and rare ferns that love the black peaty soil – The sea full of grey mysterious islands and rocks, seals and seabirds. White glistening beaches and transparent sea all the way across to Eriskay. Blue mountains of Barra to the west – and the Cuillins far away snow covered to the south – There are 5 other cottages in Glendale and no road

4 *Cheeky Chicks* 1950 (detail)

2 South glendale.
South Lochboisdale.
Isle of South Uist.

Dear Andrew –
This is the place after my heart. I wonder if you would like it. Not a tree, not a bush. But grey boulders grey rocks, grey stones, grey mountains. and bog in between – In the bog lochs with water lilies, and rare ferns that love the black peaty soil. The sea full of grey misterious Islands and rocks, seals and sea birds. White glitering beeches and transparent sea all the way across to Eriskay. Blue mountains of Barra to the west. and the Coolins far

nearer than 3 miles – one comes by boat and then walks – The [McInnes] family consists of a father and mother crofters, 3 sailor sons, a daughter who goes to college in Glasgow and an adopted orphan – everyone sings, everyone talks gaelic. There are 2 collies 3 puppies 2 black cats 4 cows 3 calves, innumerable hens and cocks and chickens and the point is to try to keep them out of the cottage – Peat fire, water carried from a well, everything as primitive as you want.

It was here that she painted *Cheeky Chicks* [plates 4 and 6], named after the chicks who kept trying to come into the cottage. This painting shows Winifred's preferred composition, of flowers in a container placed in the foreground with a beautiful view in the distance, in this case out towards Eriskay. There is a delicate balance between far and near held together by the bright and warm colours. A variety of brushstrokes, from the dabbed impasto of the chicks to the zigzag of

5 Letter from Winifred Nicholson to her son Andrew

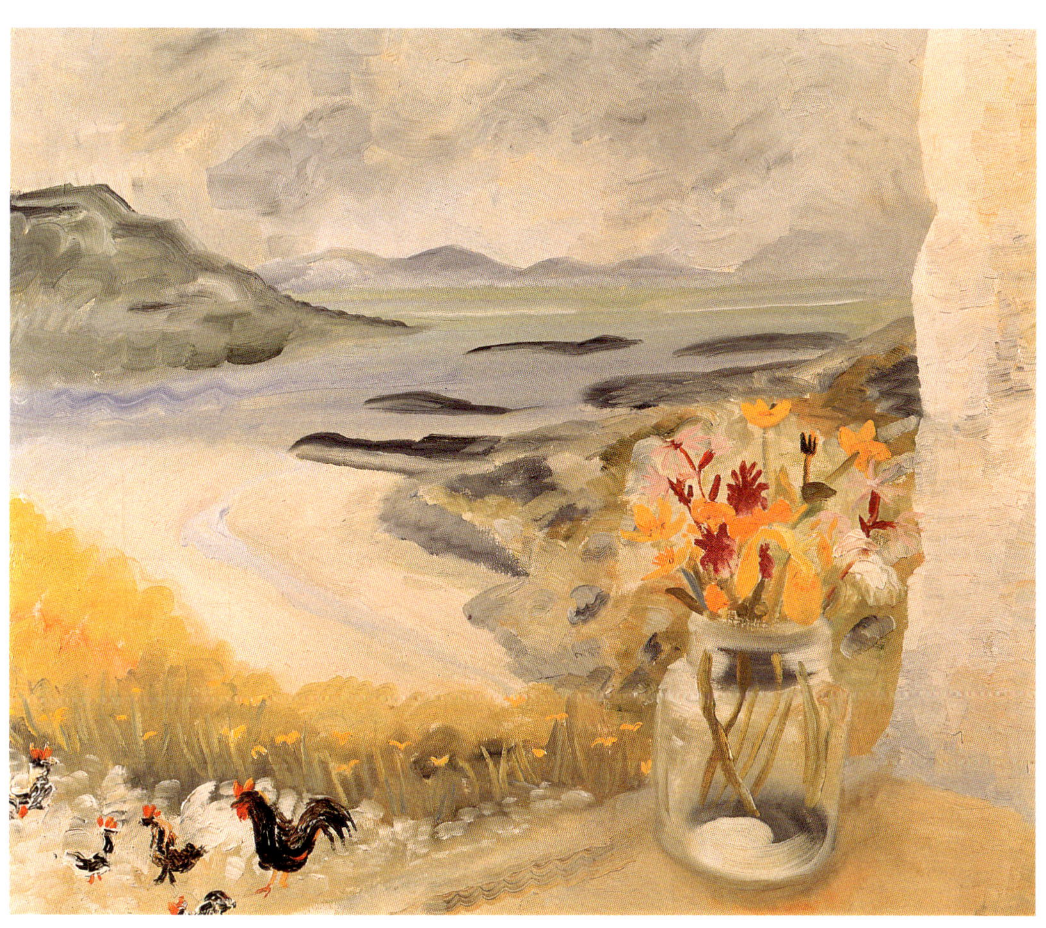

6 *Cheeky Chicks* 1950
Oil on canvas · 62 x 75cm · Private Collection

aquamarine in the water, centre left of the picture, animate the surface of the painting. Winifred depicts the warm sunlight of an idyllic summer's day in a work infused with happiness, joy, humour and a sense of the ethereal.

Winifred is mainly known as a painter of flowers, but the reason she chose this subject matter was that she felt, of anything in the world, flowers best conveyed light and therefore colour, the concern at the heart of her work. She explained:

Colour is seen in growing things, living the life of the rainbow curve, the sevenfold spectrum. Flowers create colours out of the light of the sun, refracted by the rainbow prism. So I paint flowers, but they are not botanical or photographic flowers. My paintings talk in colour and any of the shapes are there to express colour but not outline. The flowers are sparks of light, built of and thrown out into the air as rainbows are thrown, in an arc.[11]

She continued: *I like painting flowers – I have tried to paint many things in many different ways, but my paint brush always gives a tremor of pleasure when I let it paint a flower – and I think I know why this is so. Flowers mean different things to different people – to some they are trophies to decorate their dwellings (for this plastic flowers will do as well as real ones) – to some they are buttonholes for their conceit – to botanists they are species and tabulated categories – to bees of course they are honey – to me they are the secret of the cosmos.*[12]

Winifred was fascinated by the challenge of how to depict true colour. The purple orchids and golden buttercups in *Cheeky Chicks* illustrate how she once described trying to create yellow:

Yesterday I set out to pick a yellow bunch to place as a lamp on my table in dull, rainy weather. I picked Iceland poppies, marigolds, yellow iris: my bunch would not tell yellow. I added sunflowers, canary pansies, buttercups, dandelions; no yellower. I added to my butter-like mass two everlasting peas, magenta pink, and all my yellow broke into luminosity. Orange and gold and lemon and primrose each singing its note.[13]

The optimism expressed in *Cheeky Chicks* reveals how sympathetic Winifred found her surroundings on South Uist. She had a talent for adopting and enjoying the way of life of the places where she worked and was fascinated by the traditional activities of the crofters, such as the dyeing of homespun yarns. She described this in her letter to Andrew:

Everyone spins, dyes the wool with wonderful dyes from lichen, yellow iris root, waterlily root, blue or peat fire soot which makes yellow and thus weaves into beautiful tweed – I have a bit for a coat and shirt for myself … There are, over about 2 miles of bog, 2 old ladies who live in a one-roomed white cottage – thatched – they have a wonderful white calf – and a red duck, the room is full of fleeces drying after the dyeing – they can make a crotal dye from lichen off the rocks that is browner and purpler than anyone else and o what wonderful songs they sing, with this queer Hebridean cadence and modes that sound like Chinese singing – They are both very small, like fairy women, and the walls of their house are 4 ft thick – and they have soft white hair like silk and they are almost bent double with old age and their eyes are bright blue and o, the laughter and the jokes they make.

Winifred herself spun and dyed wool and cloth and was a patron of crafts in Cumberland, particularly the making of rag rugs. Kathleen Raine recalled: 'Crafts interested her no less than did painting proper, nor did she draw a line of distinction between the "fine arts" and the dyeing of fleeces in brews made of lichen and bog-myrtle collected on a walk across a moor.'[14]

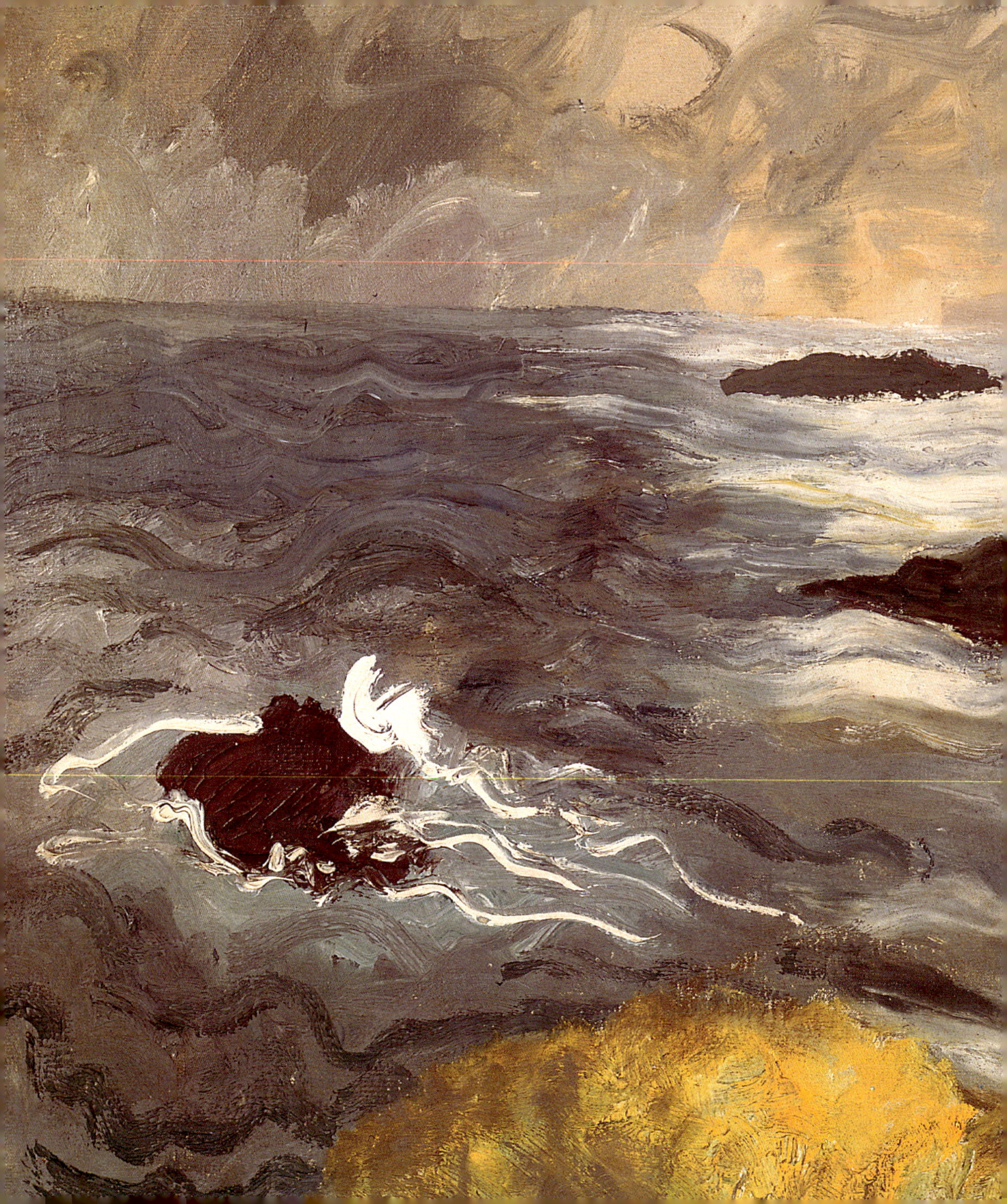

CANNA

Winifred visited Canna, known as 'the garden of the Hebrides', on at least two occasions; the first time was in July 1950 with Kathleen Raine, the second was with her son Jake in September 1951. The small, remote island was owned by John Lorne Campbell and his wife Margaret Fay Shaw, the celebrated recorders of Gaelic culture and leading nature conservationists. Winifred immediately found herself in sympathy with them and recalled their first meeting in a letter to Andrew:

Last Sunday we went to Church with the minister in Canna. It is a distance of 23 sea miles and we went as we went to Rum in the little open boat from Muck – but it was a lovely day, pale seagreen sky and deep arctic blue sea – and all the sea-birds flying and diving past us … We had lunch with the laird of Canna who is a great Celtic scholar – and collects folklore. We had all our lunch collected on the island, lobster and cream – and for pudding seaweed (carageen moss) and cream. Canna is a lovely flowery island like Eigg.

When Winifred returned with Jake in 1951 they stayed with the Campbells in Canna House, near A'Chill [plate 8]. It was during this working trip that she painted *Equinox* [plate 9] *and Isle of Canna* [plates 7 and 10]. In both paintings Winifred conveys a sense of the wild weather they withstood whilst on Canna. On this sparsely inhabited island, life is governed by the forces of nature and Winifred and Jake were prevented from leaving by violent equinoctial storms. As a result she painted both works inside Canna House, looking out of a window. In *Equinox*, the harbour, nearby Sanday and distant Rum are visible, whilst *Isle of Canna*

7 *Isle of Canna (Canna)* 1951 (detail)

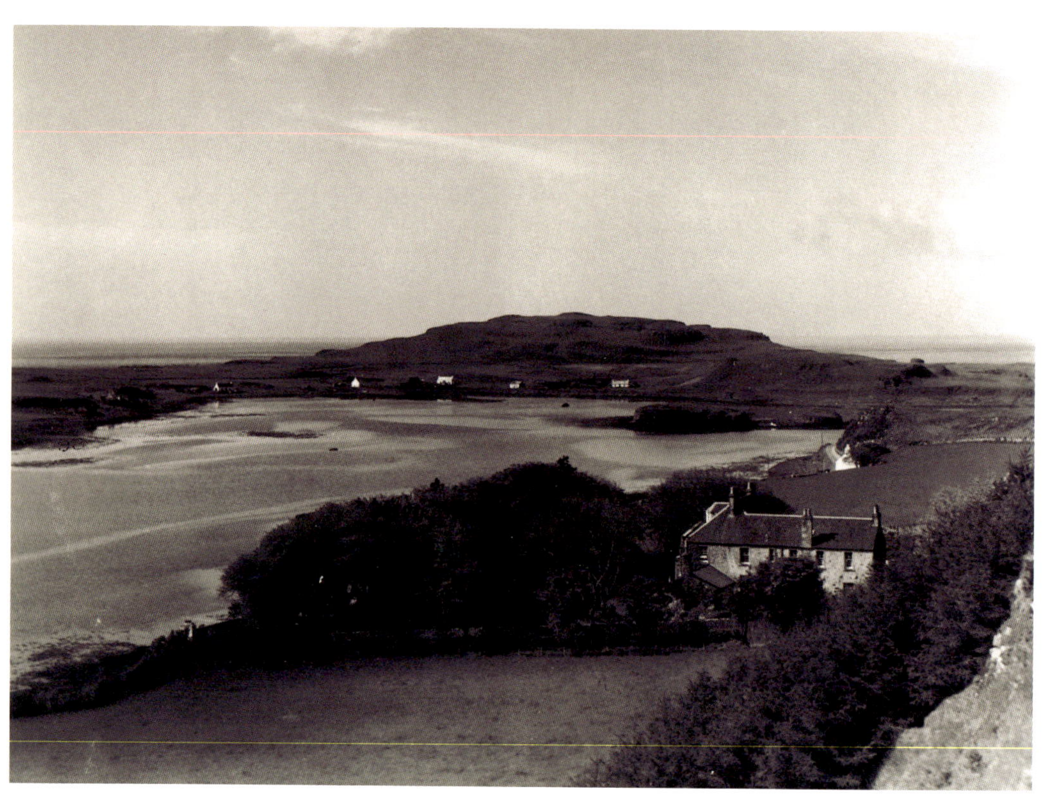

8 Canna House looking to Sanday

shows an area further along the coast, with one of Canna's headlands in the distance.

These island seascapes illustrate Winifred's fascination with the cool, silvery light of Scotland and the continually shifting effects it had on her surroundings in the frequently unpredictable weather. She liked to paint in places where light was dispersed or reflected and the atmospheric conditions and expanses of water of the Hebrides provided the perfect environment for these phenomena. She was interested in the interplay of light between water and sky, as well as trying to convey the erratic patterns of waves and their often violent meeting with land.

There is a sense of the mystical in much of Winifred's work, in particular, *Equinox* and *Isle of Canna*, which reflects her own deeply spiritual nature. She became interested in Christian Science in the late 1920s, and followed the faith in combination with her own essentially optimistic way of thinking. She considered the act of painting fundamentally uplifting and Jake Nicholson has explained that all her works are joyful as she wanted them to bring something positive to those who looked at them. Kathleen Raine summarised Winifred's spirituality:

For Winifred the eternal was not some static abstraction but a living essence of the present moment, in which she had the gift of living so fully. To that moment she brought the whole of herself to meet whatever epiphany was present before her eyes, as a gift, as it were, from the ever-flowing world.[15]

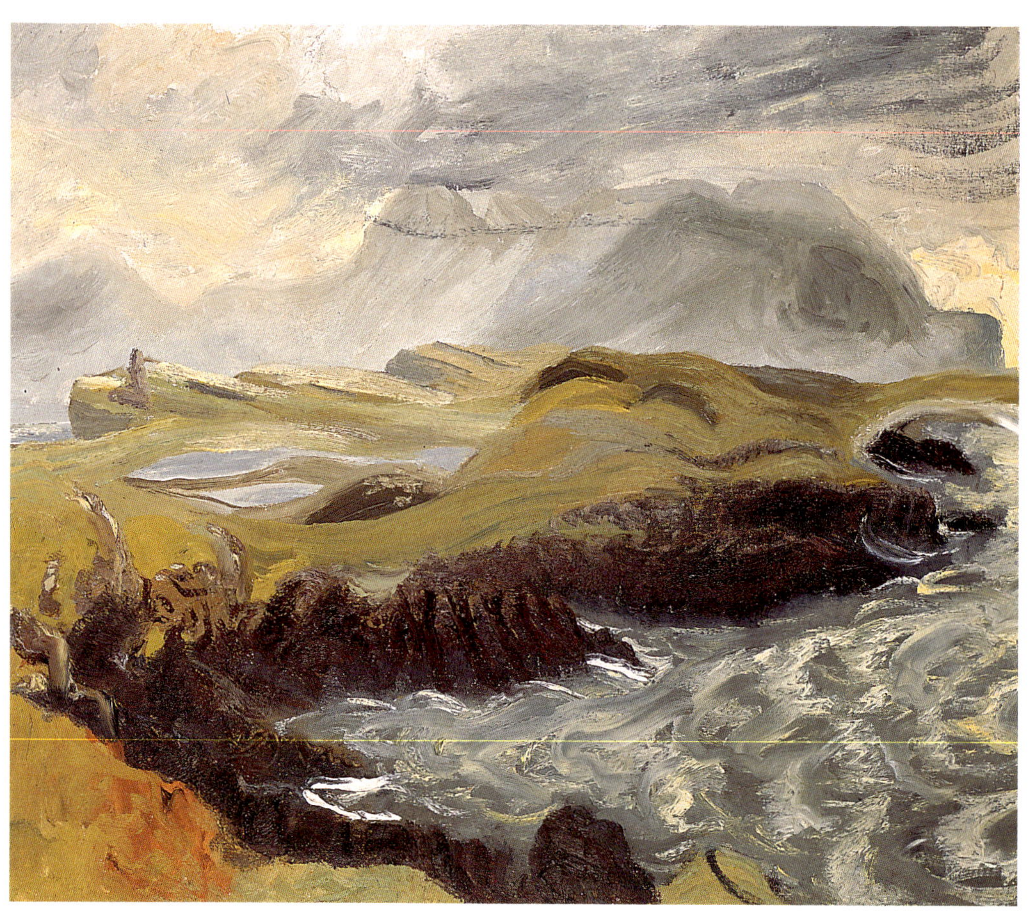

9 ***Equinox*** 1951
Oil on canvas · 63 x 76cm · Private Collection

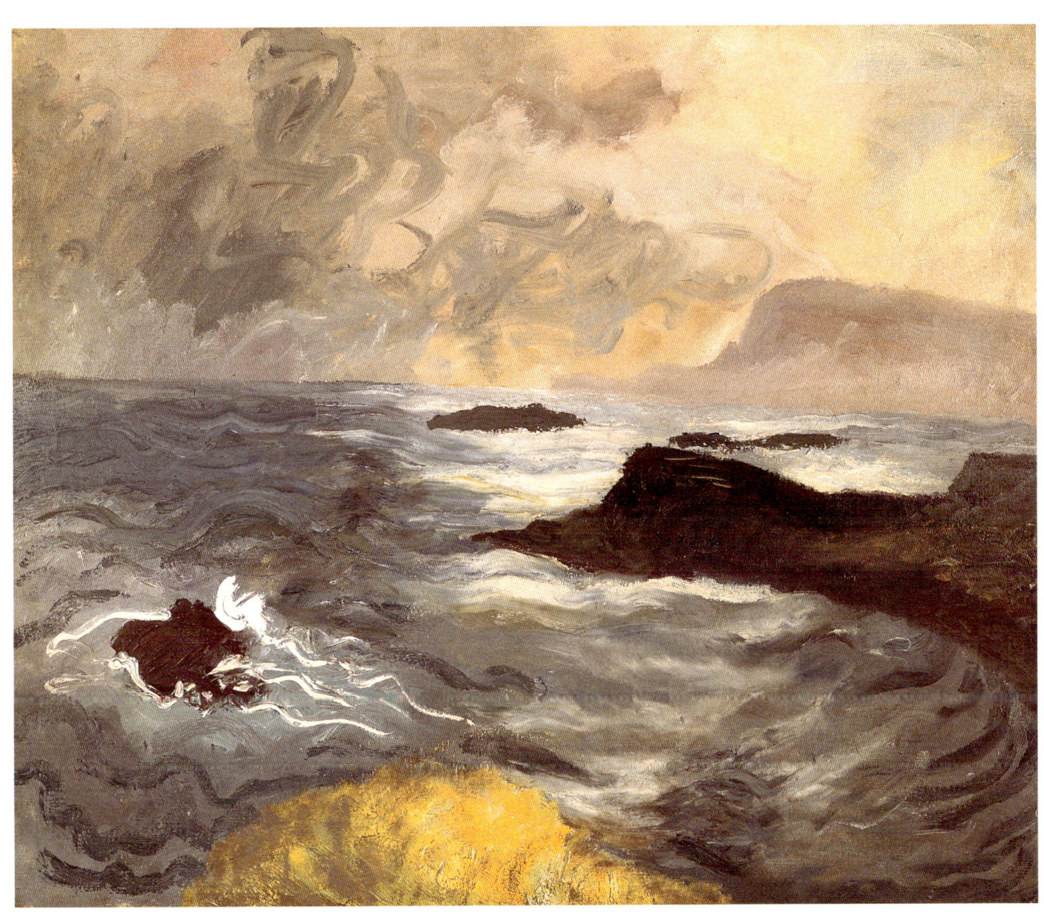

10 *Isle of Canna (Canna)* 1951
Oil on canvas · 63 x 76cm · Private Collection

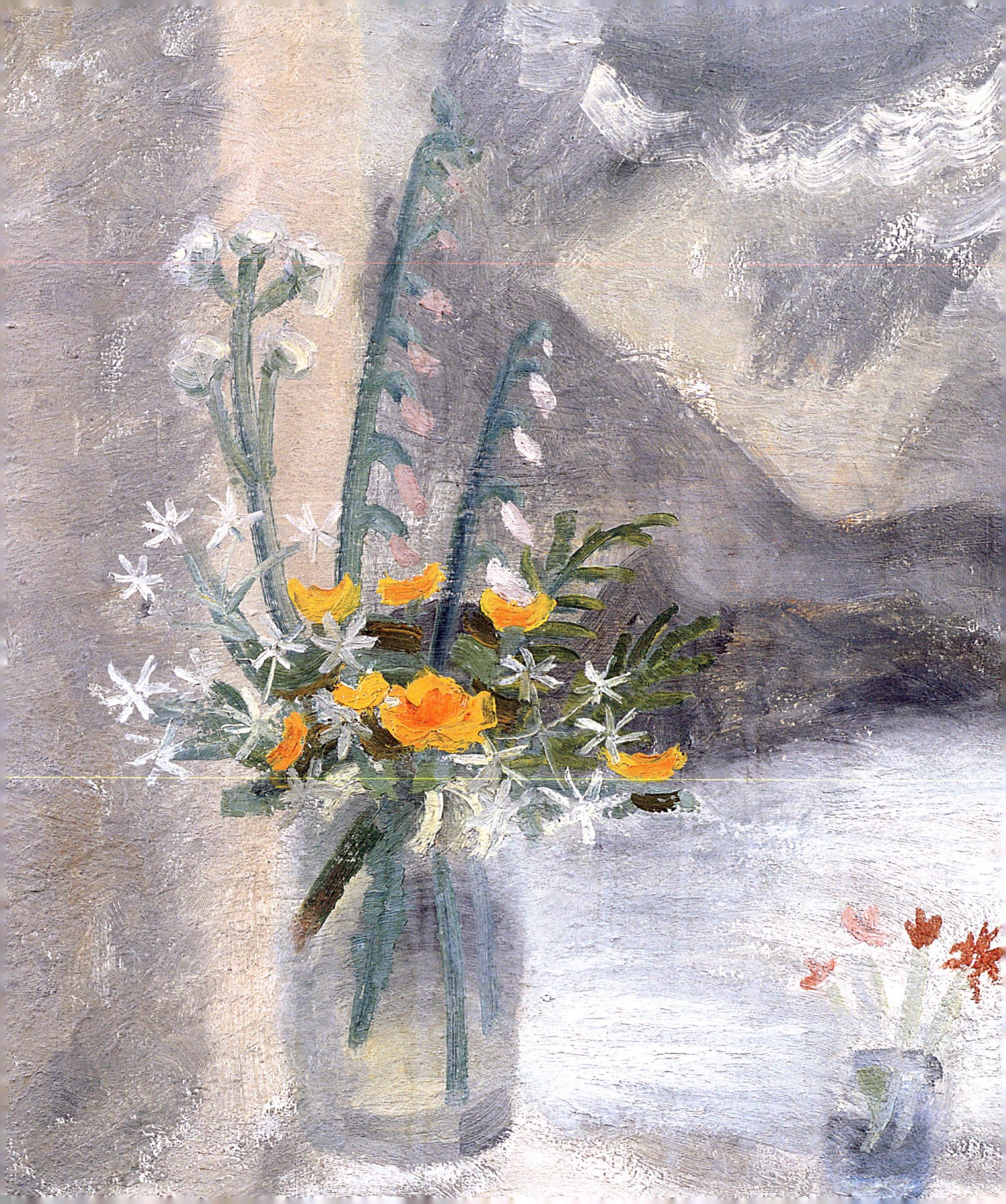

SANDAIG

One of the most important places in Scotland for Winifred was Sandaig in Ross-shire, on the west coast of the mainland. She stayed there with Kathleen Raine many times throughout the 1950s on a small croft, which they rented from the writer Gavin Maxwell, and is the place which he immortalised as Camusfeàrna in his *Ring of Bright Water* trilogy.[16] The fact that Winifred repeatedly returned to work in Sandaig with Kathleen is testimony not only to the inspiration she found in this remote and wild place of outstanding natural beauty, but also to their friendship, which lasted from 1948 until Winifred's death in 1981.

Kathleen's mother was Scottish, and she spent much of her childhood in Northumberland. She was introduced to Winifred by the sculptor, Henry Moore, at an exhibition in which he and Winifred were represented. They met again at Cockley Moor, the Cumberland home of the collector and patron of the arts, Helen Sutherland, and from that point they became friends.[17] Like Winifred, Kathleen felt a particular empathy with the natural surroundings and ancient culture of the Highlands and Western Isles of Scotland. Kathleen had met Gavin Maxwell through Tambimuttu, who was the first publisher of her poetry, and Maxwell allowed her and Winifred to stay in Sandaig when he was away. During their early visits there was no water supply, except from the nearby waterfall, telephone or electricity and there was no road to the cottage.

Kathleen described the almost sacred atmosphere that she and Winifred sensed there:

Gavin, from the wreck of his fortunes, had kept one thing; a small, shepherd's

11 *Loch Hourn* 1952 (detail)

house, on a friend's estate on a wild coast of the Western Highlands; and beyond the house, a group of little islets on the largest of which was a lighthouse.

...an island salt and bare,
The haunt of orcs and seales and sea-mew's clang

Into such an isle, so Milton tells, the mount of Paradise was changed when the man and the woman were driven away...It is even said by those who live in the Western Isles that the Gaelic speech was the language of Eden. Nor could he have known how thin the veil which there divides the visible from the radiant 'other' land whose image is mirrored on those silver seas. The very light is like a quality of the imagination – the same imagination that sings in those ancient pentatonic and hexatonic melodies that seem the pure utterance of the one mind which casts the light on the sea and raises the hills like visions.[18]

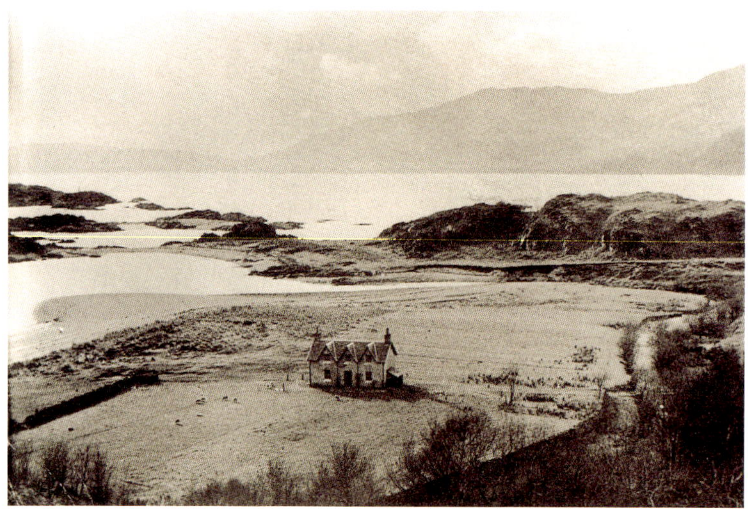

12 Sandaig, showing the ring of bright water, spring 1950

Winifred described the idyllic surroundings and way of life at Sandaig in a letter to her son Andrew:

We are on the Sound of Sleat and the mountains of Skye are opposite – Cuillins behind them … You can see the islands of Eigg and Rum out to sea, down the south to the south west – You can't in all this vast mountain land see a single human habitation except only the lighthouse keeper's house is 1½ miles away but we can't see it – after that Glenelg is the nearest house 5 miles away and Arnisdale 6 miles south. No house can be seen on Skye across the narrow deep sound. But its not a bit lonely because the animals are so friendly almost company and not scared of humans. Sheep with lambs on the small flat pasture around us – rabbits on our threshold, cuckoos on the chimney pot – bats <u>in</u> the chimney – eiderduck that talk softly in human slightly surprised voices. Sandpipers everywhere nesting in the sand banks – Eagles in the sky – wood warblers in the dingle by the waterfall don't stop singing when one goes to fill one's buckets – sandpipers don't stop looking for things in the sand while one collects the driftwood with which we make our fire. – Kathleen loves playing 'Stone Age' which means that we have nettle soup, collect mussels off the rocks – and cockles and razorfish – and she goes out fishing with the lighthouse keeper and his 3 boys … But its really very comfortable and snug – the house is warm and sheltered: 2 rooms all lined ceilings and walls with pinewood. Kathleen has the kitchen and I have the other room. Very dark to paint in, but who wants to paint indoors in this lovely weather… the boys of the lighthouse keeper come down the hill each day with our post – but if anything spectacular happens in the world, do tell me for we have no newspaper, no wireless, and my watch has stopped … Who would live in a town?

Winifred conveyed this sense of the idyllic in paintings such as *Sandaig* [plate 13] and *Bonnie Scotland* [plate 14].[19] In contrast to her depiction of

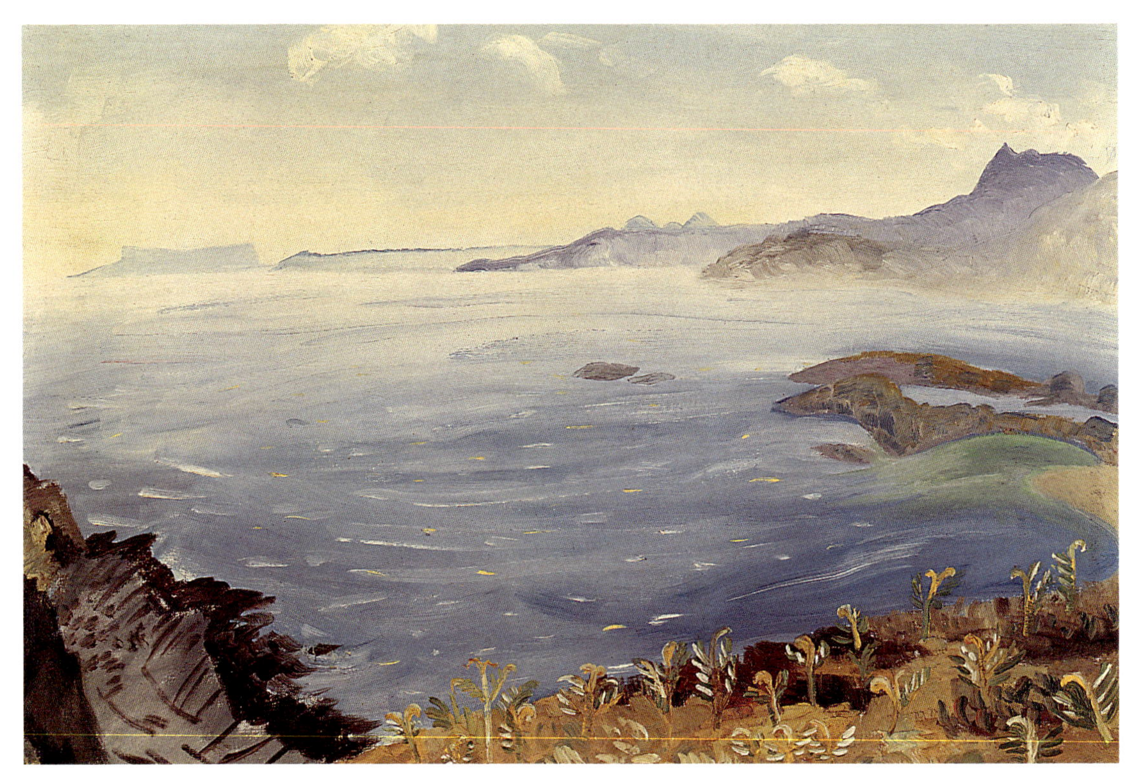

13 *Sandaig* 1951
Oil on canvas · 61 x 91cm · Private Collection

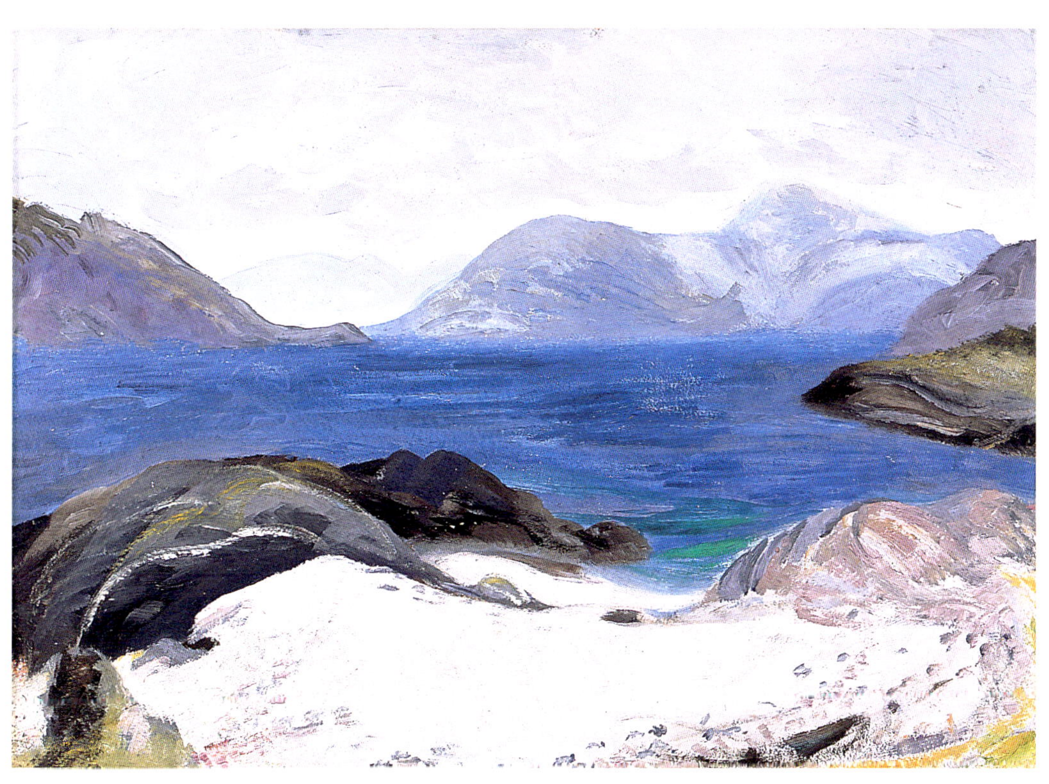

14 *Bonnie Scotland* c.1951
Oil on board · 59 x 84cm · Tullie House Museum and Art Gallery, Carlisle

the stormy weather on Canna, *Sandaig*, in particular, evokes the hazy light and warmth of a beautiful spring day, with golden sunlight illuminating the almost cloudless sky and shining through the turquoise translucence of the calm sea. She painted the same view, of Eigg, Skye and the edge of the Cuillins, with the peaks of Rum in the background, in *Sea Treasures* [plate 15]. As well as gathering the flowers that grew about her at Sandaig, Winifred also collected shells from the nearby white sand beach, and in this work presents these natural riches almost as an offering to the sea and the distant islands. This painting and Kathleen Raine's poem *Shells* illustrate the closeness of the friends' response to their surroundings, one expressing their emotions in oil paint, the other in words:

SHELLS by Kathleen Raine

Reaching down arm-deep into bright water
I gathered on white sand under waves
Shells, drifted up on beaches where I alone
Inhabit a finite world of years and days.
I reached my arm down a myriad years
To gather treasure from the yester-millennial sea-floor,
Held in my fingers forms shaped on the day of creation.

Building their beauty in the three dimensions
Over which the world recedes away from us,
And in the fourth, that takes away ourselves
From moment to moment and from year to year
From first to last they remain in their continuous present.
The helix revolves like a timeless thought,

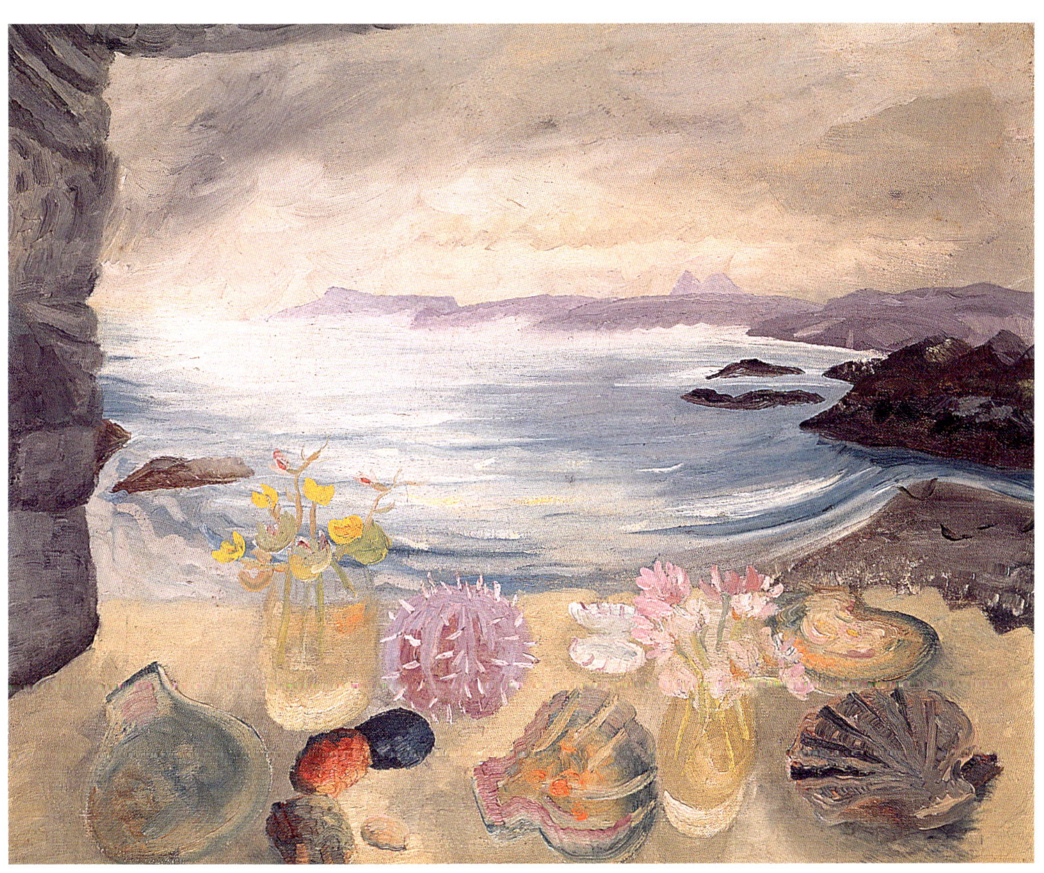

15 *Sea Treasures* 1952
Oil on canvas · 60 x 76cm · Private Collection

Instantaneous from apex to rim
Like a dance whose figure is limpet or murex, cowrie or golden winkle.

They sleep on the ocean floor like humming-tops
Whose music is the mother-of-pearl octave of the rainbow,
Harmonious shells that whisper for ever in our ears,
'The world that you inhabit has not yet been created.'

Kathleen recalled working with Winifred:

I knew her at work and value those times in retrospect as perhaps the happiest of my own life and the most productive. For to be near Winifred was to be with a totally committed artist, for whom each day shed its light on a new theme for a painting. The ever-changing light of the seasons, the flowers, the weather, the arrivals and departures of children and grand-children, all these gave her what she called the 'stories' of her paintings in which she captured the day, the hour, and ever-fleeting present. Every painting is such an irrecapturable moment of life – she painted fast, each canvas the work of a morning or afternoon, some worked over perhaps the next day or the day after, but never laboured over in a studio for weeks … she painted much in the open air and in all endurable weathers.[20]

Winifred and Kathleen immersed themselves into the life and spirit of Sandaig. Together they read Celtic myths and investigated the romance of Gaelic culture, with its folklore of witches, the evil eye, omens, mermaids, fairies and kelpies (malignant water spirits who took the form of a horse) as well as sacred waters, stones and trees. Growing beside the cottage, as with many Highland crofts, was a rowan tree, believed to have both protective and malignant powers, if, for example, its berries were brought into a home.[21] Winifred used lichen to dye wool, which she had spun by people who lived nearby, and knitted into garments. They made friends with other locals, including the shepherd, whom Winifred painted playing his bagpipes in *The Piper who Played the Retreat at Tobruk* [plate 16].[22]

Loch Hourn [plate 17], a painting of the sea loch south of Sandaig in which Kathleen had seen a whale spouting, epitomises Winifred's favourite composition and she wrote to Jake to explain why she returned to it time after time: 'I have been very happy painting – I like painting … but

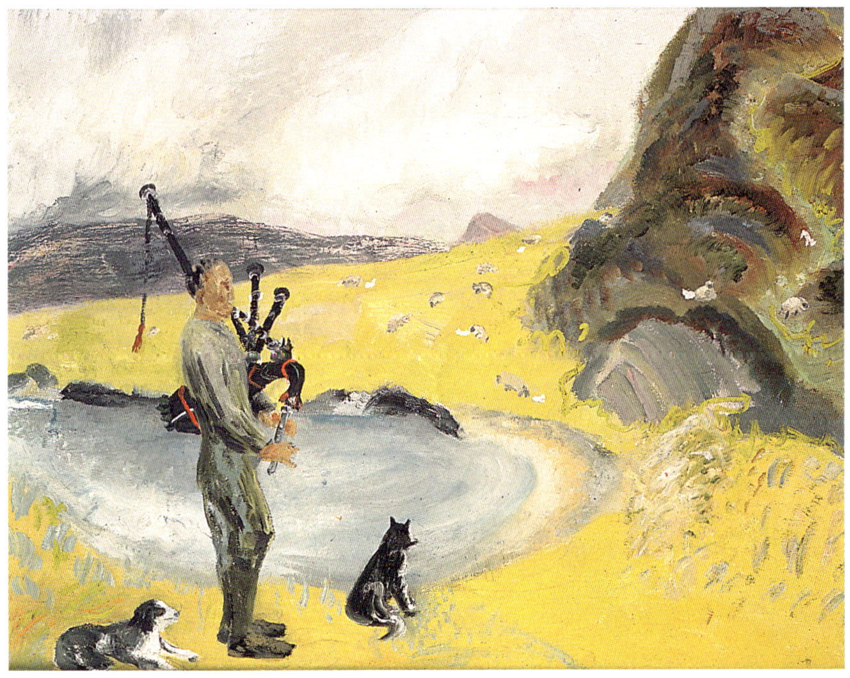

16 *The Piper who Played the Retreat at Tobruk (Shepherd, Sandaig)* c.1952
Oil on canvas · 71 x 91cm · Private Collection

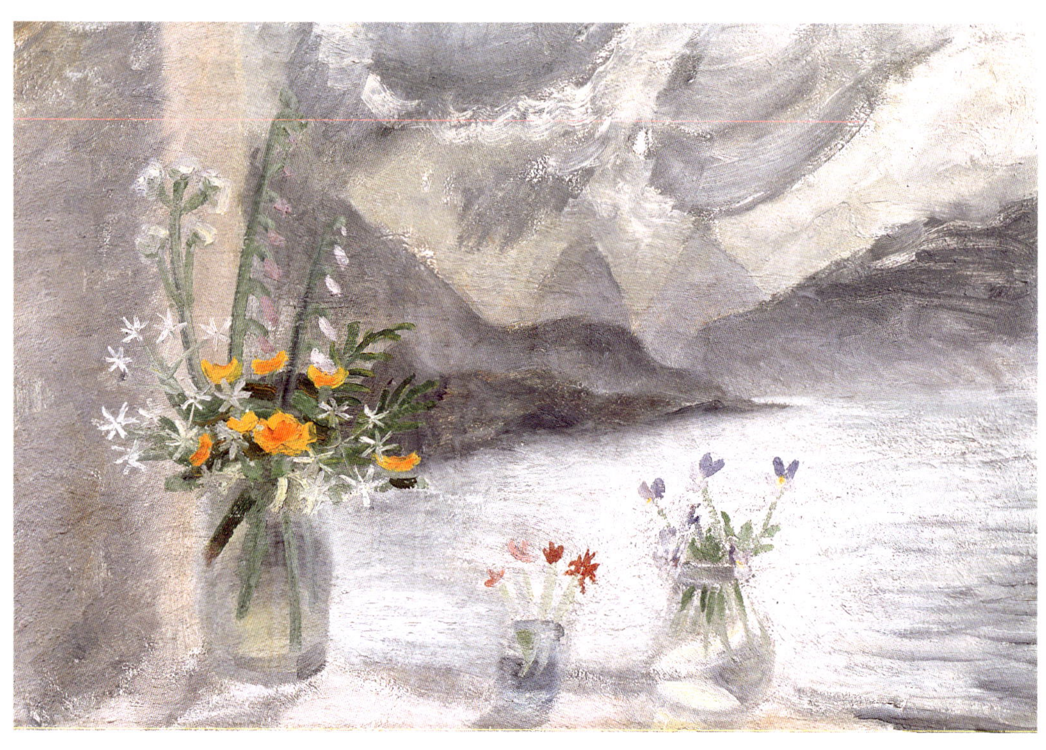

17 *Loch Hourn* 1952
Oil on canvas · 49 x 75cm · Crane Kalman Gallery, London

many of my schemes are the same ones. I find no end to them. Why seek new themes – No flowers or birds do – Why not the same – happily the same.'

Winifred's Sandaig paintings reach a climax in *View from Gavin Maxwell's* [plate 18] and *Wild Flower Window Sill* [plate 19] which show views from opposite sides of the cottage. In both she orchestrates a plethora of flowers in the foreground set before tranquil views. These works illustrate both her love of flowers, which she shared with Kathleen, and her understanding of the concept of colour. Together with mathematics and music, Winifred believed that colour was one of the three great abstract arts and she considered it analogous to human emotion. Just as maths is based on a scale from nought to infinity and music on a scale from base to treble clef, she believed that colour was based on a scale of the repeating spectrum, containing colours from red to violet, with others, as yet unknown, at either end. Moreover she understood colours as a phenomenon in their own right, free of form, which change under different light conditions and 'wish to fly, to merge, to change each other by their juxtapositions, to radiate, to shine, to withdraw deep within themselves'.[23] What she attempted to do in her paintings was to capture and express colour, rather than to represent things, because 'the local colour of an object does not belong to the object. The colour that seems to sit on it is subjective, fleeting, effervescent, and is as illusive as magic.'[24] Thus, as Kathleen explained: 'the botanical structures of flowers didn't particularly concern her although she had a wonderful gift of communicating the structure of a flower with a few brush marks … You didn't just look at the flowers, you received a whole atmosphere, meaning, quality.'[25]

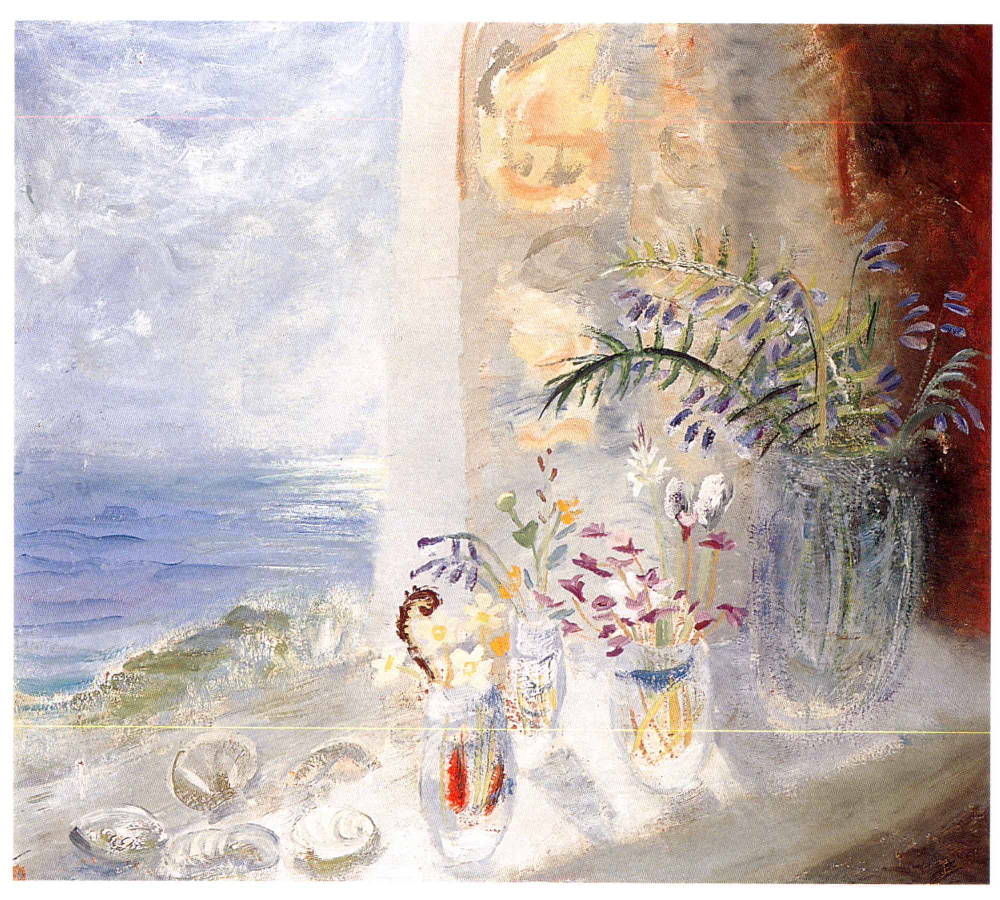

18 *View from Gavin Maxwell's* 1958
Oil on board · 57 × 69cm · Private Collection

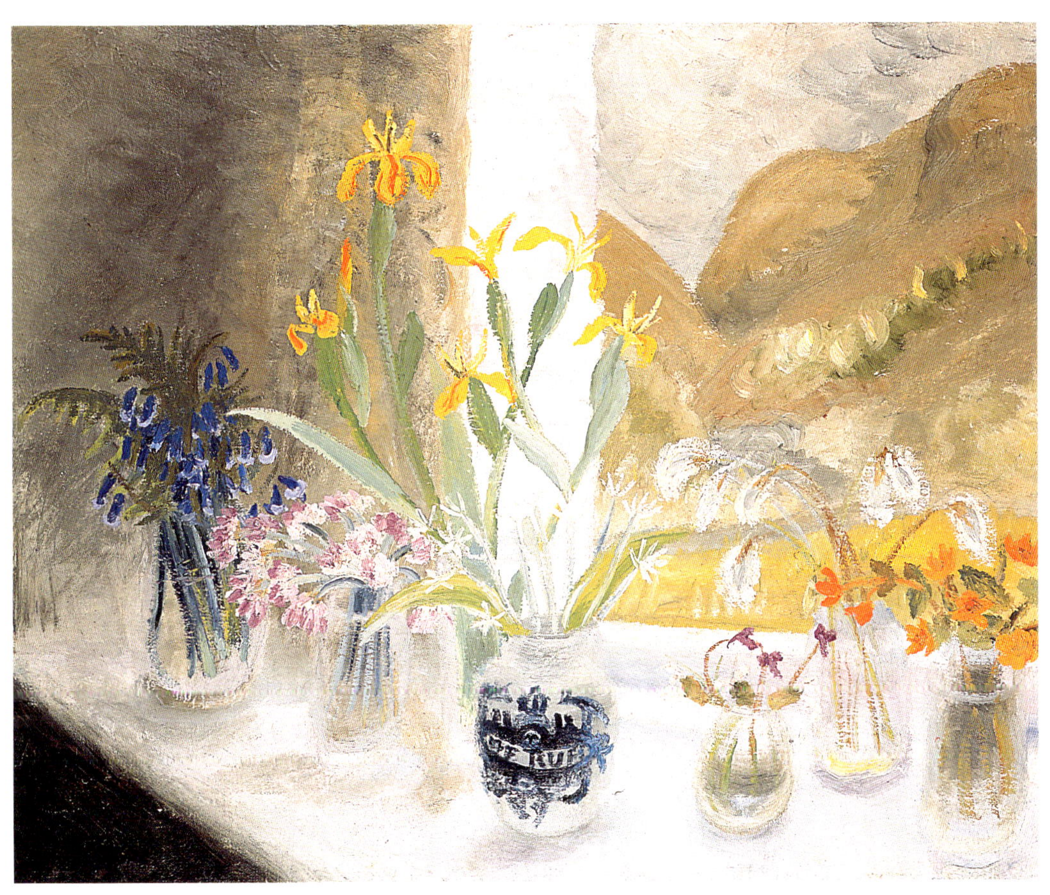

19 *Wild Flower Window Sill* 1950s
Oil on canvas · 58 x 74cm · Private Collection

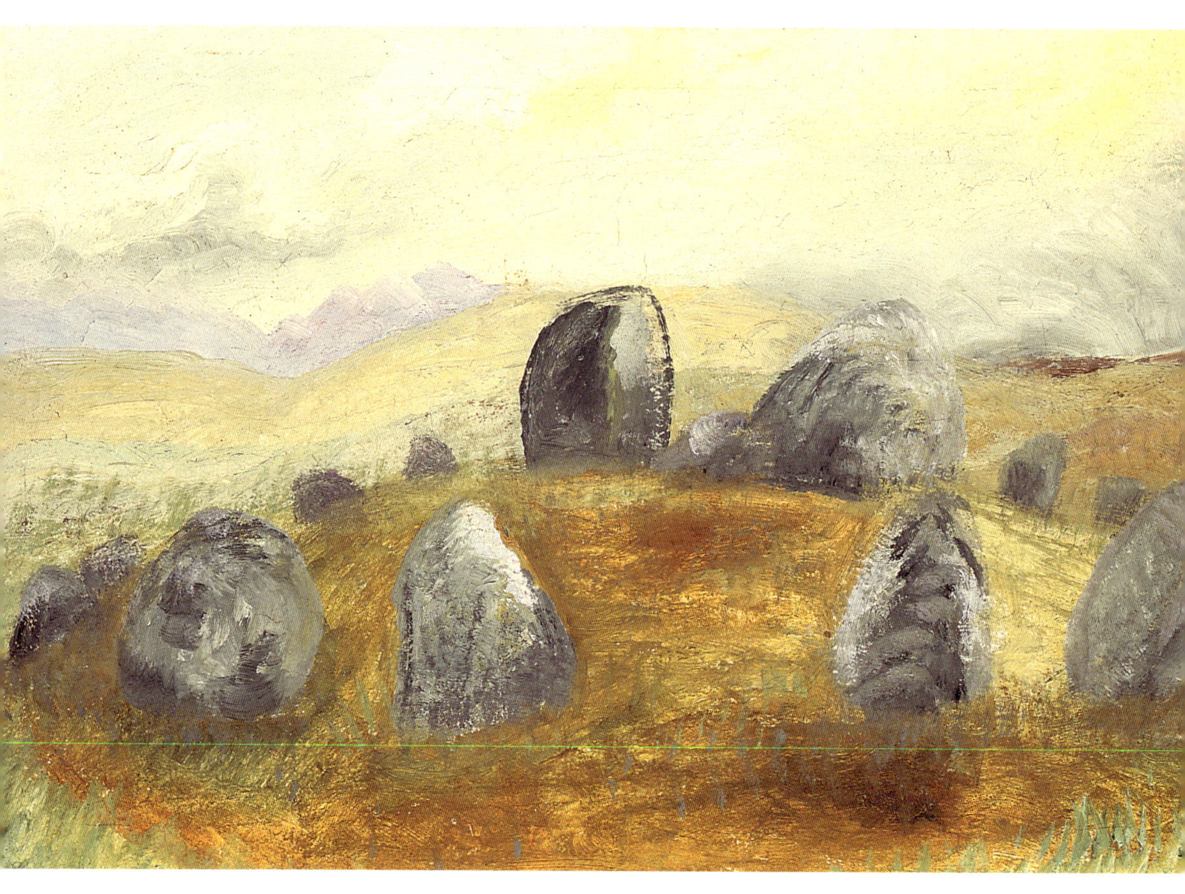

20 *Stranraer Bronze Age Circle* 1950s
Oil on canvas · 51 x 76cm · Private Collection

DUMFRIES AND GALLOWAY

Living in a house built on Hadrian's Wall, Winifred was constantly aware of the proximity of Scotland. Every time she left her home to travel west towards Carlisle she could see the Scottish hills across the Solway Firth, and they appear in the background of a number of her Cumbrian landscapes. She made frequent day trips to paint in neighbouring Dumfries and Galloway, to the Borders and was particularly fond of the Galloway coast.

Winifred is likely to have painted *Stranraer Bronze Age Circle* [plate 20] on such a day trip. Its subject has been identified as the stone circle at Torhousekie, just west of Wigtown.[26] She was deeply interested in prehistory and was drawn to archaeology as the product of an ancient civilisation whose thought was visual rather than literary.[27] Kathleen recalled: 'Megalithic stones fascinated her, in part for their "story" of a primitive human life close to the earth; but also for the shaping and placing of them, combining strength with the kind of free fluidity of line she herself knew so well how to create.'[28]

Winifred made extended visits to other parts of Scotland which are not discussed here. For example, she painted at least one other stone circle while working in Orkney during the summer of 1953. However, despite their archaeological sites she was not attracted to the ordered prosperity of the islands and felt that they lacked the creativity of the Western Isles. She explained in a postcard to Jane Harrison, Jake's future wife: '[They] are very modern and prosperous with the most up-to-date chicken farms, happy hard working people but with no music or crafts.'

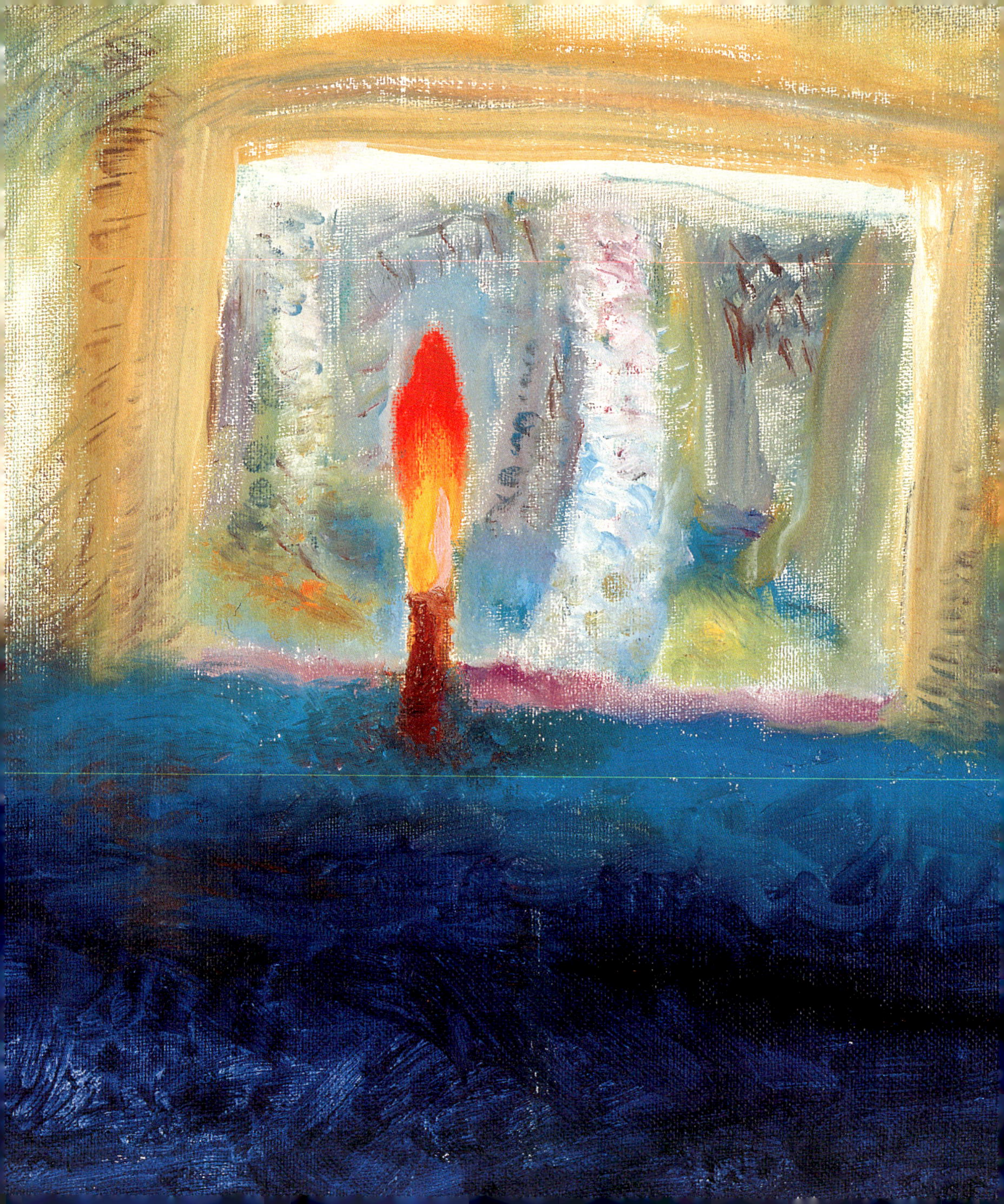

EIGG

Thirty years separate Winifred's first and last known stays on Eigg; the first visit was with Kathleen from June until July 1950. The last, which was to be her final working trip, was with her daughter Kate in May 1980. They were accompanied for the first week by the artist, Donald Wilkinson and his family and for the second by the artists, Valerie Thornton and Michael Chase. In 1950 Winifred and Kathleen stayed in the manse at night, but during the day worked in a crofter's cottage at Kildonnan. Kathleen recalled:

The Factor [of Eigg] was previously employed by Winifred's father at Boothby and he allowed us to camp during the day in an uninhabited cottage where Winifred painted and I wrote, or walked off gathering flowers, many of which Winifred painted. The croft was at Kildonnan, site of an early Christian chapel and a hermit (St. Donan) martyred by (I suppose) Norse invaders. We boiled water and made ourselves cups of tea from time to time and enjoyed the illusion of living there … On our first visit to Eigg I remember it was sultry summer weather and we walked to the top of the island where Winifred painted a canvas that was invisible because [it was] so thickly covered with midges. Several days later it was possible to brush these off, and the painting was revealed. Winifred was deterred neither by midges nor storms.

On Eigg, the tragedy of the nineteenth-century clearances of many of the Western Isles was apparent in numerous ruined cottages and other traces of previous habitation. Winifred and Kathleen walked to Cleadale in the north of the island, Eigg's only surviving group of crofts and it was near here that Winifred painted *Sound of Rum from Bay of Laig, Isle of Eigg*

21 *Candle, Eigg* 1980 (detail)

[plate 23].[29] Winifred described to Jake their involvement with the life of the island and how conducive they found it to their work:

Last Sunday the service was in our own island. It was in Gaelic which was very beautiful – rolling sad musical bible phrases – We are going to a ceilidh on Friday evening - dancing to the bagpipes and Gaelic songs. They are going to dance (men only) the war dance of the men of Eigg … Kathleen has written some magical poems. I've done about 16 pictures here, how good I don't know until I get back to look at them against other things.

Love Spell

By the Travelling wind,
By the restless clouds,
By the space of the sky,

By the foam of the surf,
By the curve of the wave,
By The flowing of the tide,

By the way of the sun,
By the dazzle of light,
By the path accross the sea
Bring my lover.

22 An extract from *Love Spell* by Kathleen Raine, Eigg, 1950
Transcribed by Winifred Nicholson

Winifred wrote in a notebook some of the poems that Kathleen composed whilst they were on Eigg in 1950, which she kept for the rest of her life. They include *Spell of Creation*, *Spell to Bring Lost Creatures Home* and *Love Spell* [plate 22].

Between her first and last visits to Eigg, Winifred travelled abroad extensively, on working trips. Throughout the 1960s she painted in Greece, with Kate, as well as in North Africa, Tunisia and Morocco, where she investigated a much

LOVE SPELL by Kathleen Raine

By the travelling wind
By the restless clouds
By the space of the sky,

By the foam of the surf
By the curve of the wave
By the flowing of the tide,

By the way of the sun
By the dazzle of light
By the path across the sea,
Bring my lover.

By the way of the air,
By the hoodie crow's flight
By the eagle on the wind,

By the cormorant's cliff
By the seal's rock
By the raven's crag,

By the shells on the strand
By the ripples on the sand
By the brown sea-wrack,
Bring my lover.

By the mist and the rain
By the waterfall
By the running burn,

By the clear spring
By the holy well
And the fern by the pool
Bring my lover.

By the sheepwalks on the hills
By the rabbit's tracks
By the stones of the ford,
Bring my lover.

By the long shadow
By the evening light
By the midsummer sun
Bring my lover.

By the scent of the white rose
Of the bog myrtle
And the scent of the thyme
Bring my lover.

By the lark's song
By the blackbird's note
By the raven's croak
Bring my lover.

By the voices of the air
By the water's song
By the song of a woman
Bring my lover.

By the sticks burning on the hearth
By the candle's flame
By the fire in the blood
Bring my lover.

By the touch of hands
By the meeting of lips
By love's unrest
Bring my lover.

By the quiet of the night
By the whiteness of my breast
By the peace of sleep
Bring my lover.

By the blessing of the dark
By the beating of the heart
By my unborn child,
Bring my lover.

brighter and stronger light than that which she found in Scotland. In 1980 when Winifred returned to Eigg and its more gentle light, she was concerned that it might have become over-modernised. She had met Donald Wilkinson in 1975, at an exhibition of his work at the LYC Museum and Art Gallery, Brampton, of which she was a patron. Donald, his wife Shirley and their children Luke and Anna had stayed on Eigg in 1979 in the Gamekeeper's Cottage, and they invited Winifred and Kate to return with them the following year. Having read the brochure about the cottage Winifred wrote to Shirley:

What do we cook on? And see by, after dark? When I was there we cooked on peat – and saw by candles, but by this brochure they seem to have civilised it – I hope they have not spoiled it – Its charm was that it was un-spoilt – and untrampled – I have a car which we could take if two of you, Donald and yourself, would like to drive – I could get a friend to drive Kate and me and I hope a lot of pictures, back.

On Eigg, at the age of eighty-six, Winifred created a vigorous late body of work. The Gamekeeper's Cottage is the highest house on the island, with panoramic views across the sea to the mainland. Due to the atmospheric conditions in the area, rainbows occur there with unusual frequency. From an early age Winifred had been fascinated by them, as they were a natural display of the splitting of light into the colour spectrum. She explained:

As a child and ever since, I have painted rainbows – the mathematics of colour, their sequence as time in painting as in music or the multiplication table, their appearing and disappearing as unreal as myth or fairytale. Who can find the pot of gold at the rainbow's foot where it touches earth? Who can see the colour at either end of the rainbow beyond ultra-violet and infra-red?[30]

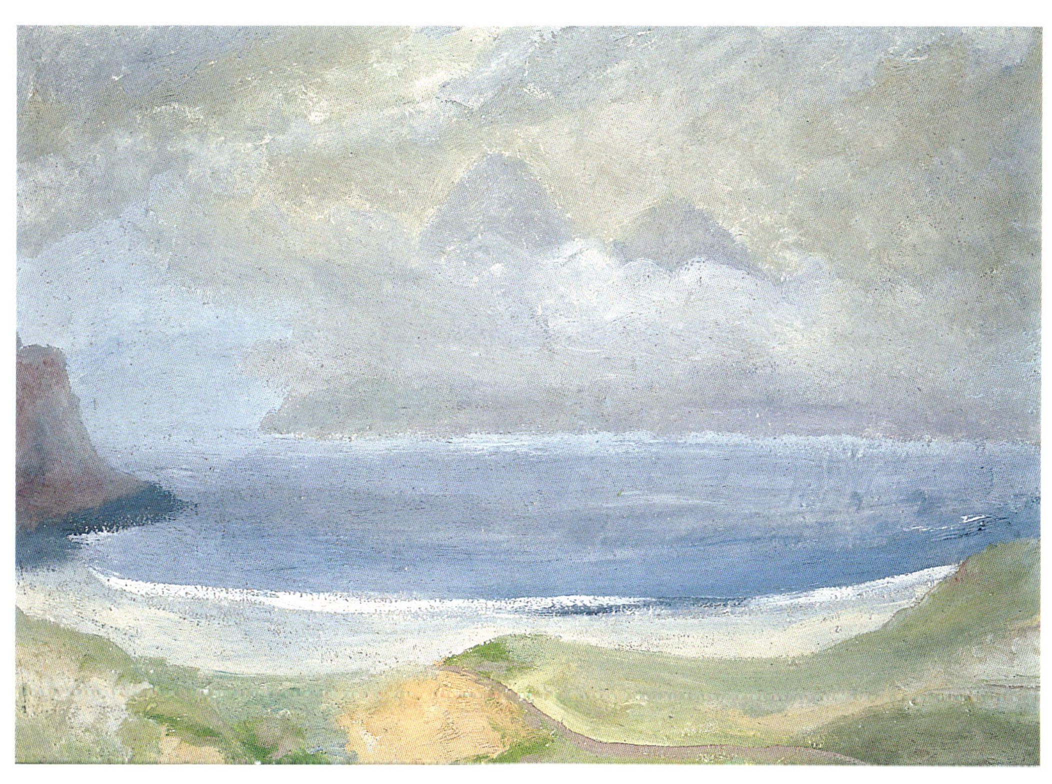

23 *Sound of Rum from Bay of Laig, Isle of Eigg (The Singing Sands)* early 1950s
Oil on board · 62 x 87cm · Private Collection

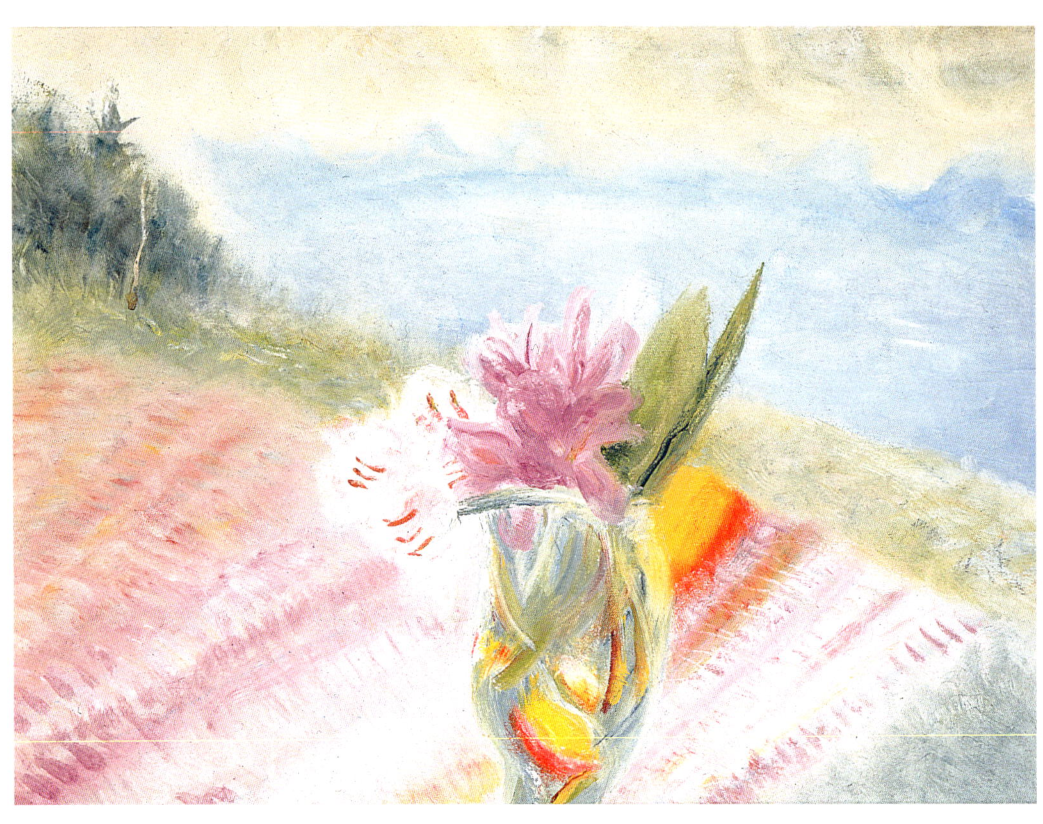

24 *Rhododendrons, Eigg (Pink Rhododendrons)* 1980
Oil on canvas · 45 x 61cm · Private Collection

In 1975 Winifred met Professor Glen Schaefer, a Canadian physicist and biologist, who encouraged her to purchase two prisms. She could look through them and see the same division of light into colour as appears in a rainbow, confirming her personal colour theory, which she summed up as 'how form is related to colour – colour is not just a coat over objects – it lies on the rim of objects between one form and the neighbouring form or space'.[31]

As a result, during this final working trip, Winifred was able to combine her deeply felt love of Scotland and fascination with the light there, with her lifelong concern for colour and the edges of the visible spectrum. In works such as *Rhododendrons, Eigg* [plate 24] and *Hebridean Roses, Eigg* [plate 25] she looked through a prism in order to paint flowers, picked on the island, which created the spectrum of light caught in the glass vessels. In both works she set the flowers before seascapes which shimmer with northern spring light. Donald Wilkinson believes that these paintings perfectly encapsulate the brightness and stillness of the peaceful days on which they were made. He watched Winifred at work and recalls how she painted in an immediate and fluent manner, working directly from nature [plate 2]. She propped up her canvas or board, on a chair, table or on the ground, preferring to work on a domestic scale as she intended her pictures to be hung in living rooms rather than in public galleries. She spent a great deal of time looking at the colours of her subject and mixing paints on her palette to create the creamy consistency that she favoured. After suggesting the main areas of the eventual composition in, for example, crayon, she would make the gesture of brushstrokes with a clean brush before loading it with paint which she applied in confident, vigorous strokes, working intuitively, at speed and in deep concentration.

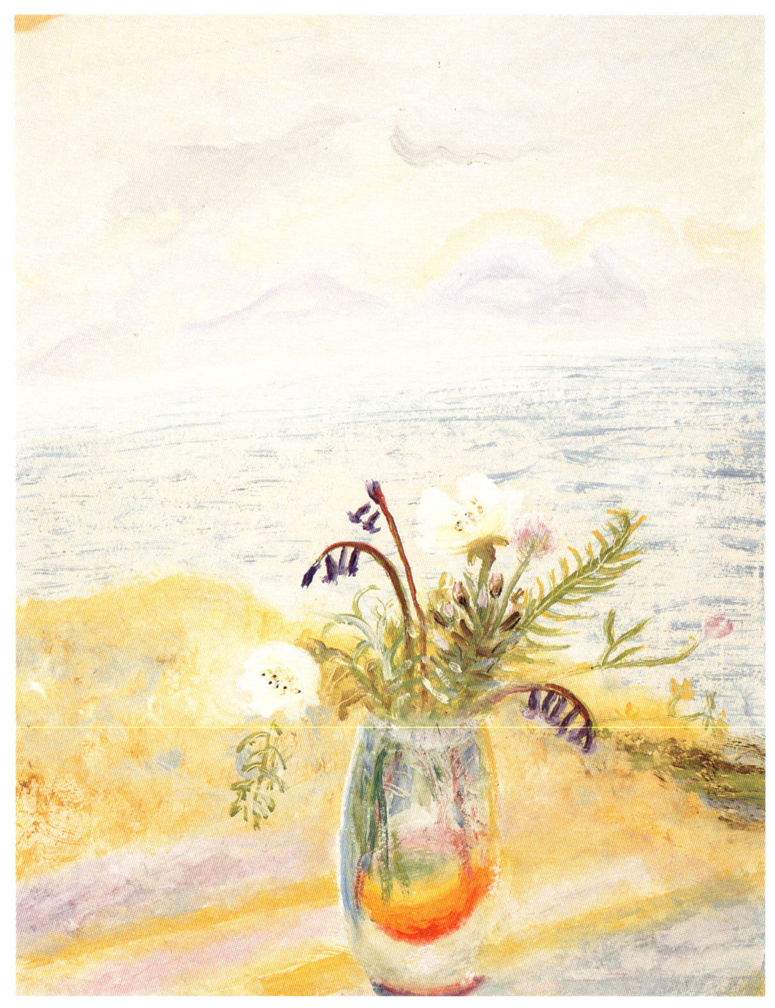

25 *Hebridean Roses, Eigg* 1980
Oil on card · 56 x 45cm · Private Collection

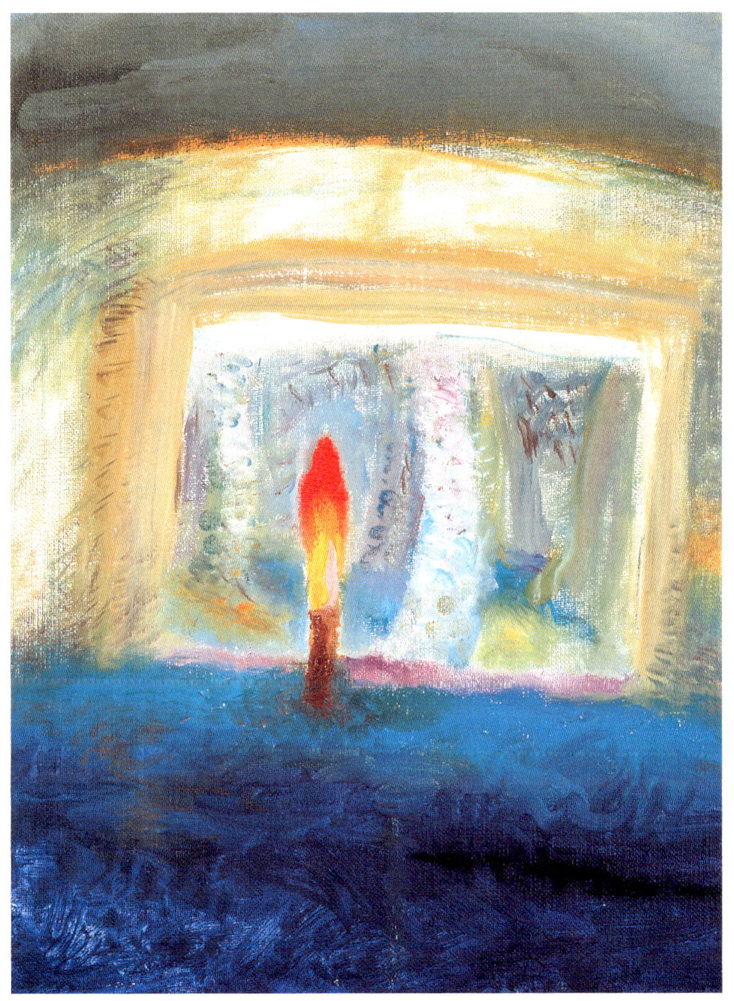

26 *Candle, Eigg* 1980
Oil on canvas · 62 x 46cm · Private Collection

If the results were not satisfactory, she simply painted over the image or turned the canvas around to use its other side.

Winifred had developed this method of working partly as a practical way of combining painting with the raising of her three children, believing the roles of mother and painter to be complementary. She reserved the morning, which she considered a sacred time, for working, and dedicated the rest of the day to her children and other domestic responsibilities. When not working with Kathleen, Winifred was always accompanied to Scotland by at least one of her children. Jake and Kate, who are also artists, would spend their days painting, while Andrew enjoyed sailing, climbing and walking in the hills. Whilst on Eigg, Winifred was particular to make time to play with the Wilkinsons' children, Luke and Anna, each evening.

Winifred painted the mystical *Candle, Eigg* [plate 26], in her bedroom in the Gamekeeper's Cottage and Valerie Thornton recalled:

One very dark morning, Winifred said she was going to paint in her bedroom, which was very small, and darkened, even on a bright day, by a grove of larch trees outside the small deepset window. She insisted that she did not want to work in the light sitting room. When I went into the trees later, to get some wood for the stove, I understood. Burning in the window was a candle! At the end of the day there was a very potent and beautiful painting.[32]

The Gate to the Isles [plate 27] expresses the joy and optimism which Winifred maintained throughout her life and contains the element of spirituality which was at the heart of her personality. The gate marked the boundary of the Gamekeeper's Cottage garden [see plate 28]. The title refers to the Highland myth in which the souls of the dead go west to the Islands of the Blest, to live in paradise with the gods.[33]

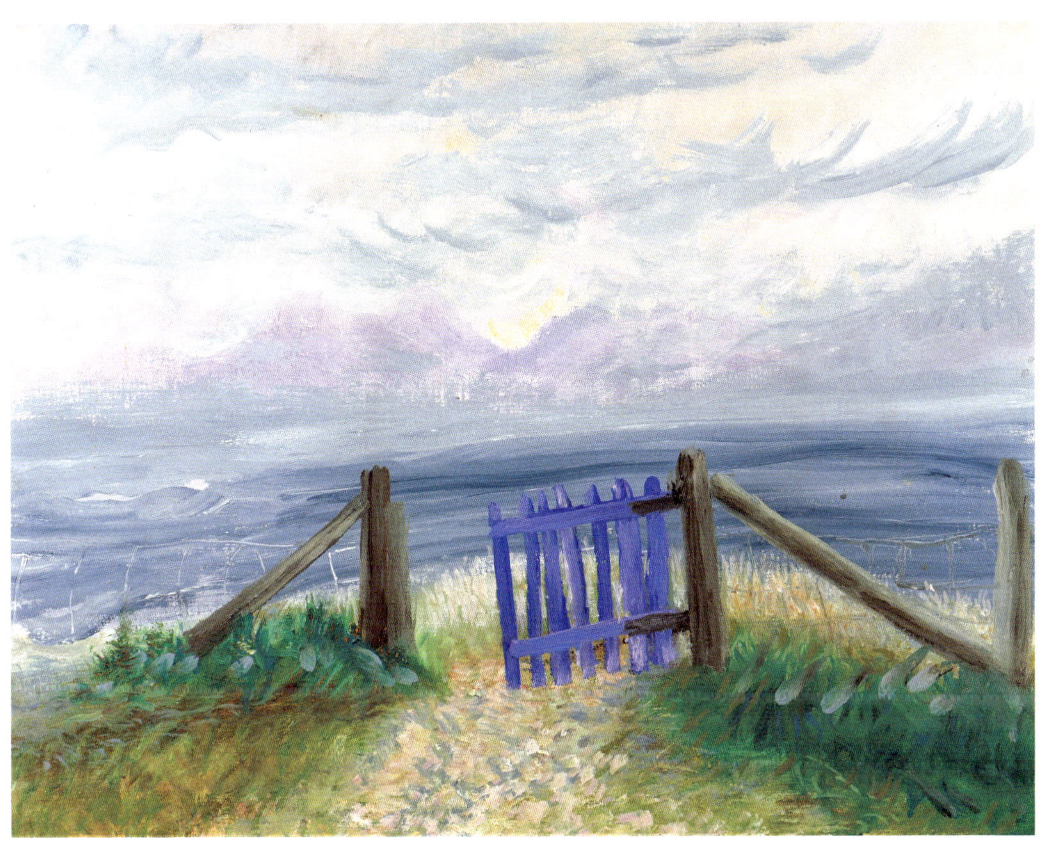

27 *The Gate to the Isles (Blue Gate)* 1980
Oil on canvas · 46 x 61cm · Private Collection

CONCLUSION

Many of the paintings Winifred made on Eigg in 1980 were included in an exhibition of her work at the Crane Kalman Gallery, London, which opened on 24 March 1981. Winifred had died three weeks earlier, on 5 March. Her repeated working trips to Scotland from the late 1940s and throughout the 1950s, and her final stay on Eigg at the end of her life, reflect her love of northern light, and the outstanding natural beauty of the Scottish landscape. She felt a deep affinity with the way of life and culture of the remote Highlands and Western Isles.[34] Scotland, in particular Sandaig, provided inspiration and a conducive environment where she could work in harmony with her children or her cherished friend, Kathleen Raine. Her Scottish paintings encompass the main concerns of her work, namely light, colour and radiance expressed through the motif of flowers and the exploration of the extraordinary phenomenon of the rainbow. Moreover, the profound spirituality of her Scottish seascapes, in which she probed the essence of light in nature, prove her to be far more than the flower painter that she is known as to many. Her lifelong optimism and openness to new ideas is shown by the exuberant works she made on Eigg in 1980, many with the use of a prism, a recently acquired painting aid. Indeed she intended to return to the island with the Wilkinsons, who had booked the Gamekeeper's Cottage for Whitsun week 1981.[35] Working in Scotland suited Winifred and she made some of her most beautiful paintings there. Several of her Scottish works, including *The Gate to the Isles* and *Candle, Eigg* are considered to be amongst the best she ever made.

Winifred explained to Kathleen that she had experienced three epiphanies in her work, one of which occurred on Eigg:

Yes the time at Eigg was a glimpse through and so was a time I had with Ben at Lugano and a time I once had in Paris with myself. I've got accustomed to glimpses-through to vanish and leave nothing but a bittersweet memory behind – which the pictures or poems that were born then only make more poignant.[36]

Winifred considered Scotland a magical place and she hoped to communicate this in her paintings. She recalled:

One may find oneself, almost without knowing it, in the Hebrides, without any effort standing by the sea and smelling the scent of heather, peat and bog asphodel – little transparent pools with pale cowrie shells – the flight of the goose across and away – the flag iris look like yellow moons in the twilight – and the – O dear me I'm almost there.[37]

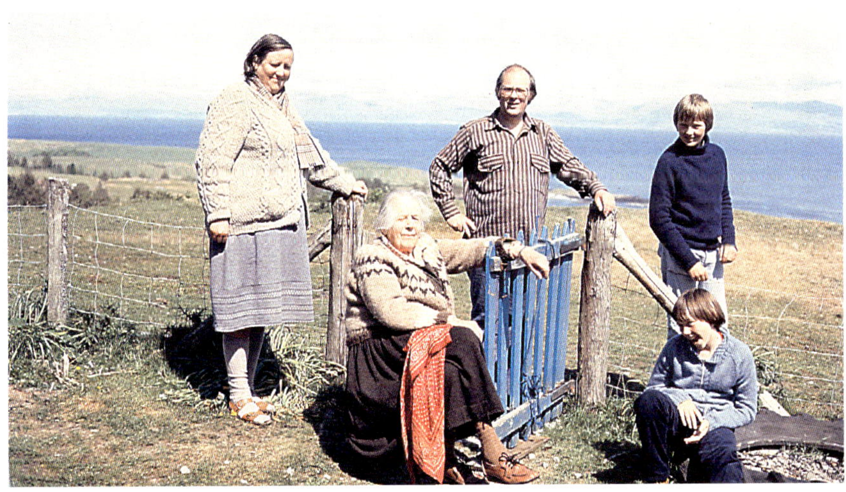

28 Kate and Winifred Nicholson, with Donald, Luke and Anna Wilkinson by the blue gate, Eigg, 1980

AUTHOR'S NOTE

Winifred rarely specified the titles and dates of her paintings. She believed that what was important about her work was the viewer's response to it and enjoyment of it, while she herself preferred to live in the present rather than to dwell in the past. She went so far as to explain: 'Dates – I hardly ever put them or remember them – I *never* sign my pictures. If I did either of these things, dates and geographical places, what would it leave for art historians or collectors to do?'[38] She only occasionally dated her letters. As a result, it is very difficult to establish exactly when, where and with whom she spent time in Scotland, whilst her Scottish paintings, in common with a number of her works, sometimes have more than one title and uncertain dates.

Much of the information in this book is based on a notebook and undated letters written by Winifred, which are in private collections, and on interviews conducted with Rafaele Appleby, Joan Halbert, Andrew, Jake and Jovan Nicholson and Donald Wilkinson, as well as letters to the author from Andrew and Jake Nicholson and Kathleen Raine.

This publication is not intended as an exhaustive survey of Winifred's time in Scotland and of the works she made there. Rather, it covers a selection of her trips and paintings and the author hopes to convey something of Winifred's love for Scotland and her individual artistic talent.

The Trustees of the Winifred Nicholson estate invite owners of works by the artist to contact Alice Strang at the Scottish National Gallery of Modern Art, Belford Road, Edinburgh EH4 3DR with regard to the compilation of a catalogue raisonné.

SELECT BIBLIOGRAPHY

BLACKWOOD 2001
Jon Blackwood, *Winifred Nicholson*, Kettle's Yard, Cambridge, 2001

COLLINS 1987
Judith Collins, *Winifred Nicholson*, Tate Gallery, London, 1987

MAXWELL 2000
Gavin Maxwell, *Gavin Maxwell: The Ring of Bright Water Trilogy* (ed.) Austin Chinn, London, 2000

MURPHY 2001
Alan Murphy, *Scotland: Highland and Islands Handbook*, Bath, 2001

NICHOLSON 1979
Winifred Nicholson, 'Blinks', *Winifred Nicholson Paintings 1900–1978*, Third Eye Centre, Glasgow, 1979

NICHOLSON 1987
Winifred Nicholson, *Unknown Colour: Paintings, Letters, Writings by Winifred Nicholson*, (ed.) Andrew Nicholson, London, 1987

RAINE 1987
Kathleen Raine, 'Winifred Nicholson's Flowers', *Temenos*, no.8, April, 1987

RAINE 1991
Kathleen Raine, *Autobiographies*, London, 1991

RAINE 2000
Kathleen Raine, *The Collected Poems of Kathleen Raine*, Ipswich, 2000

ARCHIVAL MATERIAL

Letters from Winifred Nicholson to Ben Nicholson, Tate Gallery Archive, London, TGA 8717.1.1.1696–1947

Crane Kalman Gallery Archive, London

NOTES

1. Unless otherwise stated, quotations are taken from Winifred Nicholson's letters and postcards, which were seldom dated, and a letter from Kathleen Raine to the author, 23 November, 2002.

2. Collins 1987, p.13.

3. Nicholson 1987, p.105.

4. Blackwood 2001, p.12.

5. The Earl of Carlisle, *A Picture Song Book*, London, 1910.

6. This work has also been known as: *Flodigarry Island, Isle of Skye* in *The 16th Annual Exhibition of Local Art*, City Art Gallery, Carlisle, 1949, *Island in the Sea* in the Helen Sutherland Collection no. HSC 168, *Flodigarry Island* in *Winifred Nicholson and Vivancos*, Lefevre Gallery, London, 1952, *Flodigarry* in *Paintings by Winifred Nicholson*, The Scottish Gallery, Edinburgh, 1953 and *A Highland Island* in *The Helen Sutherland Collection*, Scottish National Gallery of Modern Art, Edinburgh, 1962.

7. Mary Sorrell, 'Winifred Nicholson', *The Studio*, vol. 148, no. 736, July 1954, p.23.

8. Nicholson 1987, p.99.

9. Nicholson 1987, p.101.

10. Nicholson 1987, pp.126–7.

11. Nicholson 1987, p.239.

12. Nicholson 1987, p.216.

13. Nicholson 1987, p.126.

14. Nicholson 1987, p.197.

15. Nicholson 1987, p.199.

16. The exact dates of Winifred and Kathleen's working trips are unclear. Jake Nicholson dates the first to July/August 1949 and Andrew Nicholson has confirmed that they went throughout the 1950s. Winifred's friend Joan Halbert recalls meeting her at church in 1958 just after she had returned from Sandaig. Maxwell's trilogy consists of *Ring of Bright Water*, London, 1960, *The Rocks Remain*, London, 1963 and *Raven Seek Thy Brother*, London, 1968.

17. Raine 1991, p.266. Sutherland had met Winifred in 1925 and became an important collector of her work, acquiring, for example, *Flodigarry Island, Skye* (plate 3). Sutherland met Kathleen during the Second World War. Collins says Winifred and Kathleen met in 1948, see Collins 1987, p.38.

18. Raine 1991, p.283.

19. It is not certain that Winifred painted *Bonnie Scotland* at Sandaig.

20. Raine 1987, pp.163–4.

21. Maxwell 2000, pp.266–7 and p.319.

22. The British Army's retreat from Tobruk (Tubruq), Libya in April 1941 was followed by their recapture of the port in November 1942, bringing the battle of El Alamein to an end.

23. Nicholson 1987, p.102.

24. Nicholson 1987, p.73.

25. Collins 1987, p.30.

26. Identified by the Royal Commission on the Ancient and Historical Monuments of Scotland, National Monuments Record of Scotland site NX 35 NE 14.

27. Raine 1987, p.169.

28. Nicholson 1987, p.198.

29. This painting is also known as *The Singing Sands* after the nearby beach of Camas Sgiotaig where in certain conditions the sand makes noises when walked upon.

30. Nicholson 1979, p.7.

31. Collins 1987, p.30.

32. Nicholson 1987, p.249.

33. During a conversation in her studio, Winifred explained this to Kathleen Raine and to the owner of the painting, who bought it from the artist as a result of the visit. In various letters to Andras Kalman of Crane Kalman Gallery, London, Winifred referred to this painting by three different titles, *Blue Gate*, *Blue Gate to the Isles* and *The Road to the Isles* before settling on *The Way to the Isles*, the title under which it was shown in the Gallery in 1981. *The Gate to the Isles* has become established as its title since then.

34. Winifred had at least two solo exhibitions of her work in Scotland while she was alive. The first, *Paintings*

by Winifred Nicholson, was held at The Scottish Gallery, Edinburgh in 1953 (where she is believed to have held other exhibitions, but as the relevant records no longer exist their dates cannot be verified). The second, *Winifred Nicholson Paintings 1900–1978*, was organised by the Third Eye Centre, Glasgow and toured to Edinburgh, Carlisle, Glasgow, Newcastle-upon-Tyne, Colchester and Penwith from 1979 until 1980.

35. Kate went with the Wilkinsons, who stayed for a week. She was joined for a further week by Winifred's grand-daughter Rafaele and her friend Arlene Munro. Rafaele, a painter herself who worked with Winifred for six months in Cumberland before attending art school, was as taken with the island as her grandmother had been and returned to live there for almost two years.

36. Nicholson 1987, p.206.

37. Nicholson 1987, p.210.

38. Collins 1987, p.73.

PHOTOGRAPHIC CREDITS

Photography by Prudence Cuming, London, Keith Pattison, Gateshead and Guy Pawle, Carlisle

Detail of Ordnance Survey of Great Britain and Ireland, scale 1: 1,000,000, sheet 2, 1905. Reproduced by permission of the Trustees of the National Library of Scotland, pp. 12, 13

Jonathan Lynch Photography. pp. 20, 48

© Gavin Maxwell Enterprises, p.32

Antonia Reeve, p.7

The National Trust for Scotland
© Margaret Fay Shaw, p.26

© Donald Wilkinson, p.8

© Shirley Wilkinson, p.59